I0815169

Dreyfuss + Blackford

Dreyfuss+Blackford

Dreyfuss + Blackford

Seventy Years

ORO

ORO Editions — Novato, California

ORO Editions
Publishers of Architecture, Art, and Design
Gordon Goff, Publisher

www.oroeditions.com
info@oroeditions.com

Published by ORO Editions

Copyright © 2022 Dreyfuss + Blackford Architecture

All rights reserved. No part of this book may be reproduced, stored in a retrieval system, or transmitted in any form or by any means, including electronic, mechanical, photocopying of microfilming, recording, or otherwise (except that copying permitted by Sections 107 and 108 of the U.S. Copyright Law and except by reviewers for the public press) without written permission from the publisher.

You must not circulate this book in any other binding or cover and you must impose this same condition on any acquirer.

Project editor: Clare Jacobson
Book designer: Pablo Mandel
Managing editor: Jake Anderson

Typeset in Avenir

10 9 8 7 6 5 4 3 2 1 First Edition

ISBN: 978-1-951541-14-7

Color Separations and Printing: ORO Group Ltd.
Printed in China.

ORO Editions makes a continuous effort to minimize the overall carbon footprint of its publications. As part of this goal, ORO Editions, in association with Global ReLeaf, arranges to plant trees to replace those used in the manufacturing of the paper produced for its books. Global ReLeaf is an international campaign run by American Forests, one of the world's oldest nonprofit conservation organizations. Global ReLeaf is American Forests' education and action program that helps individuals, organizations, agencies, and corporations improve the local and global environment by planting and caring for trees.

This book is dedicated to the memory of our founders, Albert M. Dreyfuss and Leonard D. Blackford. They are Al and Len to many of us, especially those who had the privilege of working with them. The legacy they created for Dreyfuss + Blackford remains a constant reminder of our roots in modernism, and their enthusiasm for great design continues to guide our work today and into the future.

ALBERT M DREYFUSS AIA ARCHITECT

Contents

Foreword

Pierluigi Serraino

A firm's trajectory over an extended period of time results from the combination of factors. The chemistry between the founders, the energy of the collective they gather in their office, the quality of their designs, the type of clients they bring in, and being at the right place at the right time are part of that powerful mix. Ever since the founding of Dreyfuss + Blackford Architecture, these components have all been present. Through a felicitous intersection of circumstances, talent, personalities, entrepreneurship, and luck, a generalist practice was born in Sacramento, California in 1950 and grew at an exponential speed, rare even by the national standards of the era. Those same characteristics remained at the firm and, in turn, became self-propelling drivers across the workforce over multiple generations. The rewards for the company were tangible: peer recognition, financial robustness, diversity of project types, prized commissions, talent knocking at the firm's door, and more. But its longevity and relevance are possibly the most cherished achievements in its seven-decade existence. This brief historical sketch shows that the legacy of this office is essentially multidisciplinary and pluralistic. With its aim of producing long-lasting designs, the firm's quest to produce enduring designs continues to this day.

Albert M. Dreyfuss (1920–2017) and Leonard D. Blackford (1923–2014) had uncommon affinities. They reinforced each other's nature, and their mutual support became the basis of their lifelong partnership. They shared more than a professional bond. Theirs was a friendship. Their homes were close to each other. According to colleagues, they rarely, if ever, had a significant argument about the firm. They had a symbiotic relationship. Their firm's rapid growth was the organic outcome of this affinity, absent from the behavioral side effects of prima donnas. Rigid notions of division of labors were nowhere to be found. In their practice, design finesse—from conception to execution—was the result of distributed authorship, where the individuals' contributions to the project accrue to the point of becoming fused into the built outcome. They promoted and fed a culture around overall higher quality and knowledge sharing through teamwork. That same culture is present in Dreyfuss + Blackford Architecture today.

Throughout his life, Dreyfuss never forgot his small-town Louisiana roots. These roots, he said, gave him an attitude that each job was important and that he would do whatever it took to complete it to the best of his capacity. He strove to develop long-term relationships with his patrons, who became allies in the firm's ascent. In resisting the temptation to specialize in a particular building type, a business aim increasingly common in the architectural profession at the time, he set the course of the firm for decades to come.

In Blackford, Dreyfuss found his closest ally. As a Northern California native, Blackford brought a landscape sensibility to the firm's enthusiastic embrace of modernism. That formula was most impactful in adding warmth to the restrained designs of the architects' early work.

The duo's rise to prominence from their modest start was swift. Their association with John Lyon Reid, a noted San Francisco-based mid-century architect who specialized in education facilities, brought ongoing school projects that sustained the firm in its early years. In addition, occasional noneducational commissions came up. Nut Tree (1959) in Vacaville falls squarely into this category. What started as a request for a masterplan turned into a detailed project where leisure, shopping, and play found a distinctive postwar graphic sense and spatial synthesis.

The Sacramento Municipal Utility District (SMUD) Headquarters (1960) constitutes a breakthrough for the office both in its structural challenges and the demands of its design. The two young architects, accustomed to wood frame construction, exhibited impressive mastery designing large-scale buildings using the steel skeleton. That milestone marked the beginning of a run of distinctive modern buildings. In January 1966 Dreyfuss & Blackford Architects made the pages of *Fortune* magazine, where the Asclepius Medical Offices (1964) were featured next to the works of Richard Neutra and Victor Christ-Janer. Their projects were also included in the legendary *Arts & Architecture* magazine as well as in *Architectural Record* and *Architectural Forum*.

The founders designed more than a few single-family residences throughout their careers. Prior to the start of the partnership, Al Dreyfuss was the architect of the Home of Tomorrow, a

Electri-Living Home, 1957.

prototype single-family residence targeted for the middle class showcasing the latest advances in kitchen appliances and careful orientation for maximum environmental benefit. In 1952, the Freedom Gas Home was another demonstration project featuring the amenities and mechanical advancements symbolic of comfort on postwar California. In 1957, Dreyfuss & Blackford's special relationship with SMUD led to the firm's participation in the then well-known Electri-Living Home program sponsored by *Living for Young Homemakers* magazine, which solicited residential prototypes along the West Coast by notable designers. Among the other participants providing innovative ideas for homes were Palmer & Krisel in Los Angeles and Paul Hayden Kirk in Seattle. In Sacramento, Dreyfuss & Blackford designed a compact single-family home where artificial lighting played a decisive role in the occupants' quality of living. This comprehensive investigation of the newly mechanized California home demonstrated the range of design exercises the firm engaged in.

In confronting increasingly larger buildings with more complex programs, the firm needed to master the skills of managing human and material resources in order to retain the quality of its designs. Its work on the expansion of the San Francisco Airport was one such occasion. Dreyfuss + Blackford's broad proficiency allowed it to handle building types of widely different sizes with ease. Its community was formed from a tradition of thoughtful application of design principles, as opposed to specialization that can lead to creative atrophy. Invariably, such operational choice prompts a process of cyclical changes in design responses to specific problems, yet firmly anchored to the strong roots of the firm's origins.

Equally important, as the practice expanded its scope of work it grew philosophically and technically through cross-fertilization with artists, among them Wayne Thiebaud, and collaborations with other prominent architects, such as John Carl Warnecke, James Polshek, and Frank Gehry. These encounters were and remain opportunities to deal with a wide array of design approaches invariably informing the attitude toward the making of architecture. By expanding its design influences, the firm allowed changes to the modernist tone established in its early work. But as skills are determinants in providing competence, defending the craft of making buildings requires an inner engagement the members of the Dreyfuss & Blackford are invariably invested in.

In the most basic sense, the practice of architecture is a commitment to the present with eyes on the future and the heart in the past. That commitment is imbued with optimism: design will make the reality we all live in better. As elemental as this conviction, it feeds the design ethos of Dreyfuss + Blackford of today. Spatial clarity, rather than image, is the office's primary goal. That target is always understood as part of something bigger. This understanding led the designers to reflect on both the built and the natural environments in their designs. The firm's focus on the environment was already evident in the 1980s in the CalPERS Headquarters Lincoln Plaza North (1987). This is a skillful exercise in making a building out of landscape and hardscape. That attitude continued throughout the portfolio of Dreyfuss + Blackford works produced in the ensuing decades.

Thinking about architecture as part of an ecosystem puts it at the center of the firm's concern for the judicious handling of natural resources. This concern can be expressed in a variety of architectural idioms. For Dreyfuss + Blackford, modernism, updated with the environmental lessons learned from the disfavor the style went through, remains the response to the needs of twenty-first-century society.

The firm has remained generalist in scope and has completed or initiated a varied assortment of commissions. Its most recent projects add noteworthy designs to the culture of California's Central Valley community that contains much of their output. The State of California, 10th and O Streets Office Building (under construction), for example, with its thoughtfully considered siting and environmental systems, provides a new identity for this public institution. The arresting design of the County of Santa Clara Animal Services Center (CSCASC, 2021) features an artificial topography with folded roofs and a carefully landscaped courtyard for animals to roam free. The Museum of Science and Curiosity (MOSAC, 2021) reactivates the abandoned Power Station B (1912) by Willis Polk into a new museum complex, creating an icon for the city.

Dreyfuss + Blackford has a notable history of engagement with Sacramento. It promotes design awareness through educational venues, such as the annual AIA Central Valley Experience Architecture event and the Architecture Matters Design Forum. Teaming with the public is the common thread of all these endeavors. This outreach has proven to be mutually beneficial because it helps to clarify to the architects the extent of what they can contribute beyond designing buildings. That tradition of giving back to the community is an integral part of the practice's identity.

While technology and construction techniques are certain to change over time, the longevity of ideas is subject to altogether different considerations. Friendship, opportunities to transfer knowledge, fostering clients as patrons and allies, and working to grow artistically and professionally remain the most enduring values Dreyfuss and Blackford themselves handed down to Dreyfuss + Blackford Architecture, a legacy worthy of multigenerational consideration.

Asclepius Medical Offices, 1964.

The process of planning and writing this book has not only catalyzed deep introspection, but also allowed each of us involved to gain a more complete understanding of Dreyfuss + Blackford Architecture through the eyes of others. As the firm builds upon new generations, this understanding has become vitally important in maintaining our sense of culture.

The purpose of this book is to share the work of Dreyfuss + Blackford as well as to effectively convey our unique personality to both newer staff and those who join us in partnership as consultants or clients. A few of us at the firm have been fortunate to have had a significant overlap working with Al Dreyfuss and Len Blackford. This intersection forms an important bridge in creating an understanding of our past while informing our future. Collaborating with our two founders provided us a great learning opportunity and continues to guide our design efforts today.

Al and Len quietly built a practice around work that is founded in the tenets of modernism. Though generalist in terms of having a broad range of building types, the firm has consistently thrived and specialized when faced with projects that are highly complex and technical in nature. These are the moments that require the kind of simplicity that is found only through intensive efforts; the simplest of details are often the most difficult to achieve.

A shining example of this focus on detail is found in the design of the Sacramento Municipal Utility District (SMUD) Headquarters. Completed in 1960 and deceptively simple in plan and elevation, the building is somehow both rigidly rational yet flexible; it remains entirely relevant today. In its design, like that of the best submarine, no volume or material is wasted and no detail is overlooked. Our recent work on the SMUD Headquarters has been focused on effectively incorporating new technologies and components that address current and future cultural shifts while preserving the best qualities of the building's original design. In some ways, the story of the SMUD Headquarters parallels that of Dreyfuss + Blackford itself; both have built upon past greatness while looking to the future.

This book is built upon a framework that dives deeply into the foundational roots of Dreyfuss + Blackford, both past and current. To build an understanding around this foundation, we have developed the book in three sections: an overarching history from our beginnings to current leadership; a discussion around our approach to process and design collaboration; and a monograph of recent projects. Each of these tell a facet of our story, and collectively, hopefully, they convey our personality.

—Kristopher Barkley, AIA

Looking ahead and reflecting from within, Dreyfuss + Blackford Architecture is a project in and of itself. A new generation of creative minds challenge how we have worked together in the past. No longer defined by our founders' singular vision or individual voices, we have grown to understand that our potential is not held to a particular idiom but is unleashed through exploration. Together we seek to integrate the diverse perspectives within and beyond our storied walls.

Architecture and environmental design are a process of envisioning the future—one of infinite opportunities emboldened by diverse experiences and backgrounds. By working collectively, sometimes expanding off each other's unique perspectives and other times constructively countering them, we find new creative territory. Each project affords a chance to reinvent ourselves and discover new facets to our individual and collective prisms.

In our shared landscapes and overlapping timelines, we are driven to acknowledge our differences and celebrate our focus on what it means to be human. The word practice only begins to define what Dreyfuss + Blackford Architecture is and what we can do to design a better world.

—Jason A. Silva, AIA

SACRAMENTO SAVINGS
SACRAMENTO SAVINGS · SECURITY SINCE 1874
AMERICA WEST

History

Dreyfuss + Blackford Architecture started seventy years ago with two visionary individuals who championed transformational design in Northern California. Working together and with a group of exceptional people, we produced a legacy of work that the firm continues to build upon.

The Early Years

Albert M. Dreyfuss and Leonard D. Blackford were architects who designed for a rapidly changing world. Their work focused on the primacy of structure, use of glass and steel, and the aesthetics of minimalism. At the same time, it was sensitive to creating humanistic environments and integrating site, context, and landscape into design.

After graduating high school at fifteen, Dreyfuss attended Tulane University in New Orleans before going on to the University of Illinois. During these years, the Second Chicago School of Architecture and the Bauhaus were gaining influence within academia and in the practice of design of contemporary buildings in larger cities. In 1950 Dreyfuss opened his own office in Sacramento, a place far from his hometown of Shreveport, Louisiana. He found that expanding his practice to several building types and sectors kept his analytical mind busy and his workload constant. That diversity of practice continues today at Dreyfuss + Blackford, as does Dreyfuss's commitment to modernism, strong desire for innovation, and integration of forward-thinking sustainability.

Blackford grew up in Northern California and entered the architecture program at the University of California, Berkeley. At that time, the Berkeley design community fully embraced modernism. Under the guidance of architecture school dean William Wurster, Blackford found a passion for blurring the line between interior and exterior spaces. He met Dreyfuss when the two were neighbors, and they quickly discovered a common value in the tenets of modernism. Both had been lured to Sacramento by jobs with California's Division of the State Architect, and both felt creatively stifled there. When Dreyfuss quit to start his own practice, he encouraged Blackford to join him. After a few months of moonlighting, Blackford decided to join Dreyfuss full time.

Left to right: Founding partners Leonard D. Blackford, FAIA and Albert M. Dreyfuss, FAIA, 1960.

The two men had an extraordinarily creative business partnership. Dreyfuss quickly realized that Blackford was the stronger designer, "and the best thing I could do was to get out of his way," he said. For nearly fifty years they worked in perfect harmony, a potent balance of business acumen and creative inspiration. Dreyfuss could promise the prospective client an inspired landmark design and Blackford could always deliver it.

At the beginning of their collaboration, Dreyfuss landed several K–12 school projects in the Sacramento area, and Blackford set about planning and designing them. Blackford maintained a very rigorous discipline for high-quality construction drawings. He fully understood the importance of clear and accurate detailing, particularly for minimal modernist designs. This thoroughness, as well as a hands-on approach to construction administration, led Dreyfuss and Blackford to secure their first major project—the Sacramento Municipal Utility District (SMUD) Headquarters (1960).

Starr King Elementary School, 1953.

A Defining Moment

In 1952, a defining moment in Northern California architecture was about to happen. SMUD, a fledgling utility, agreed that building a new headquarters was an important step in establishing itself. At the time, SMUD was led by Paul Shaad, an outspoken iconoclast who the utility knew was just the man to drive an innovative solution. (SMUD's assistant general manager was James Kennedy Carr, who would also figure into Dreyfuss and Blackford's history.) Shaad established a short list of regional architects–including the office of Albert M. Dreyfuss, AIA–for the job. He liked to drop by these firms' projects unannounced. On the day he visited the Starr King Elementary School (1953), he found Blackford on the roof. Shaad was impressed with Blackford's hands-on design approach, his passion for quality, and the exactitude of his creative vision. SMUD selected Albert M. Dreyfuss, AIA to design its headquarters, based largely on Blackford's clear passion and promise.

Soon after, Dreyfuss made Blackford an equal partner, and Dreyfuss & Blackford Architects & Planners (precursor to Dreyfuss + Blackford Architecture) was born. (Note: the name of the firm at the date of its usage is employed throughout this book.) The SMUD Headquarters was thus instrumental in the history of the firm. It and other key buildings in Dreyfuss + Blackford's history are featured in this section.

Dreyfuss & Blackford's first office was a small, leased space on J Street in Sacramento. When projects and staff increased, Blackford designed a new office at the corner of 28th and I streets. As typical of the firm's modernist style, this office was devoid of ornamentation, blurred the lines between interior and exterior, and honestly expressed building materials. The office was constructed in 1963. With newly acquired work on Terminal B at the Sacramento Municipal Airfield (now Sacramento International Airport), Dreyfuss & Blackford outgrew the space before the company was able to move in. The firm quickly sold the just-completed office and proceeded with plans to construct a larger office. In 1965 it moved into the building at 3540 Folsom Boulevard, where it remains today. Designed in the International Style, this office serves as an iconic reminder of the firm's legacy.

Sacramento Municipal Utility District (SMUD) Headquarters

Sacramento, California, 1960

SMUD Headquarters was the first significant International Style modernist icon in the Sacramento region. The building incorporated forward-thinking technology that is still relevant today. Use of an active sun-shading system, carefully considered solar orientation, timeless and durable building materials, and a simple yet flexible floor plan contributed to minimizing the need for change, enabling SMUD's continuous operation of the headquarters to this day. The landscape was designed utilizing classic modernist principles and integrates the building into a park-like environment. While the structure serves as the central focal point of SMUD's campus, the landscape's curvilinear pathways, specimen trees, granite boulders, and organic sculptural berms create a "natural" environment that contrasts with the orthogonal geometry of the building. SMUD Headquarters received recognition through several national and international publications, including the *New York Times*. The building and site were listed on the National Register of Historic Places and California Register of Historical Resources in 2010. Dreyfuss + Blackford rehabilitated the SMUD Headquarters in 2019, and this work is shown in the Projects section of this book.

Sun-tracking louvers on the east facade.

Harold Wormoth and Paul E. Shaad, SMUD general manager, photographed for the building's opening.

Left: Sunken outdoor dining area.
Above: South facade at night.

Water City, Wayne Thiebaud's 1959 mosaic tile mural, under seasonally adjustable brise soleil of south facade.

North-facing wall of south wing with outdoor dining below.

Open-plan office in the north wing, where quarter-turned lighting aligns with the building's five-foot grid.

Above: Public entry lobby with luminous ceiling feature.

Left: The luminous ceiling system was used throughout ground floor areas, including this elevator lobby.

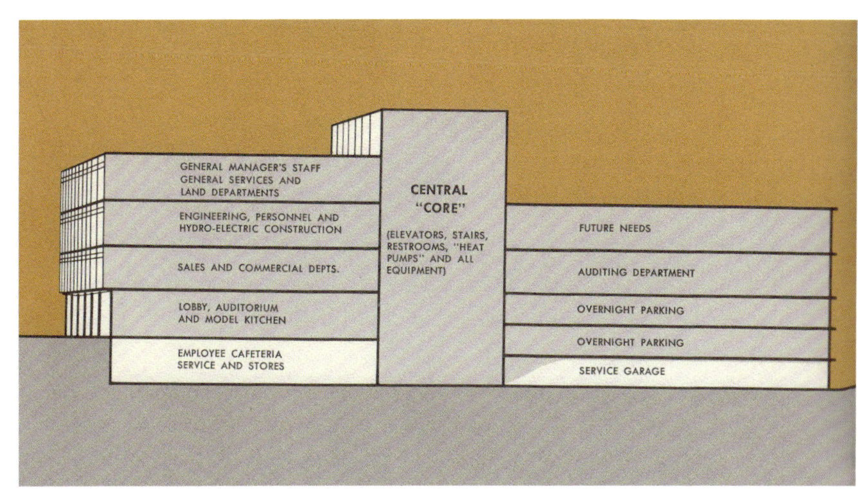
GENERAL MANAGER'S STAFF
GENERAL SERVICES AND
LAND DEPARTMENTS
ENGINEERING, PERSONNEL AND
HYDRO-ELECTRIC CONSTRUCTION
SALES AND COMMERCIAL DEPTS.
LOBBY, AUDITORIUM
AND MODEL KITCHEN
EMPLOYEE CAFETERIA
SERVICE AND STORES
CENTRAL
"CORE"
(ELEVATORS, STAIRS,
RESTROOMS, "HEAT
PUMPS" AND ALL
EQUIPMENT)
FUTURE NEEDS
AUDITING DEPARTMENT
OVERNIGHT PARKING
OVERNIGHT PARKING
SERVICE GARAGE

Above, left to right: Albert M. Dreyfuss, Leonard D. Blackford, Sophie Power, and Edwin I. Power, Jr. with scale model of Nut Tree.

Left, left to right: Albert M. Dreyfuss, Don Birrell, and Leonard D. Blackford at Nut Tree during construction.

NUT TREE

ENTRANCE
Popcorn

Nut Tree

Vacaville, California, 1959

Of all Dreyfuss + Blackford's projects, Nut Tree was its most people-oriented success. Millions of travelers stopped at the Nut Tree complex between San Francisco and Sacramento during its seventy years in business. All in one place you could get a bite to eat, visit outdoor attractions, and make fond memories. Nut Tree opened in 1921, and Dreyfuss & Blackford's work on its modernist redesign was completed in two major and several minor additions, all undertaken by the firm. The first phase, completed in 1959, consisted of a new main dining room, additions to and remodeling of a kitchen, an employee cafeteria, and a new entry canopy. The other major phase, completed in 1970, was an addition of five bays to expand the sales area, new restrooms, and administration offices. The master plan for the ranch included a general aviation airport (later donated to the city), a miniature railroad running from airport to the restaurant, restoring the original family farmhouse as a museum, and a plaza for outdoor dining. Future plans included two motels and additional restaurants. Nut Tree received an AIA Central Valley Merit Award in 1965.

View from dining area to atrium.

Richard Nixon on the Nut Tree train during his run for governor of California, 1962.

CALIFORN
1850

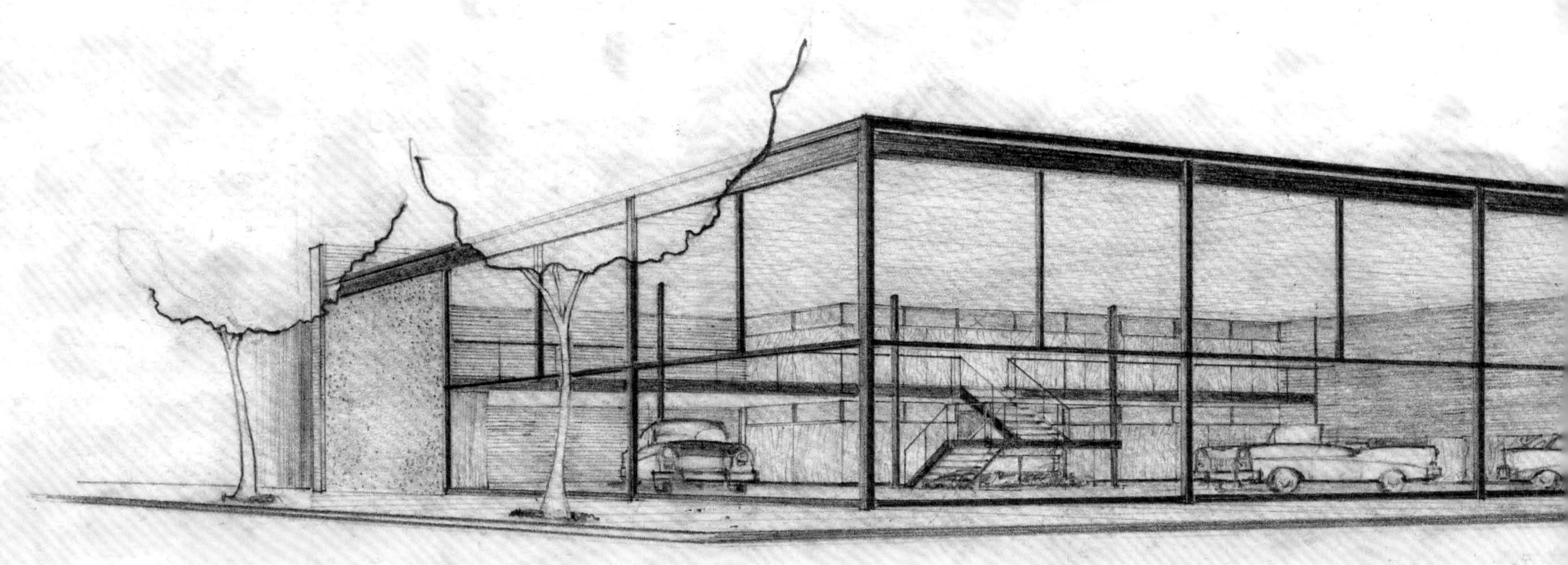
PERSPECTIVE

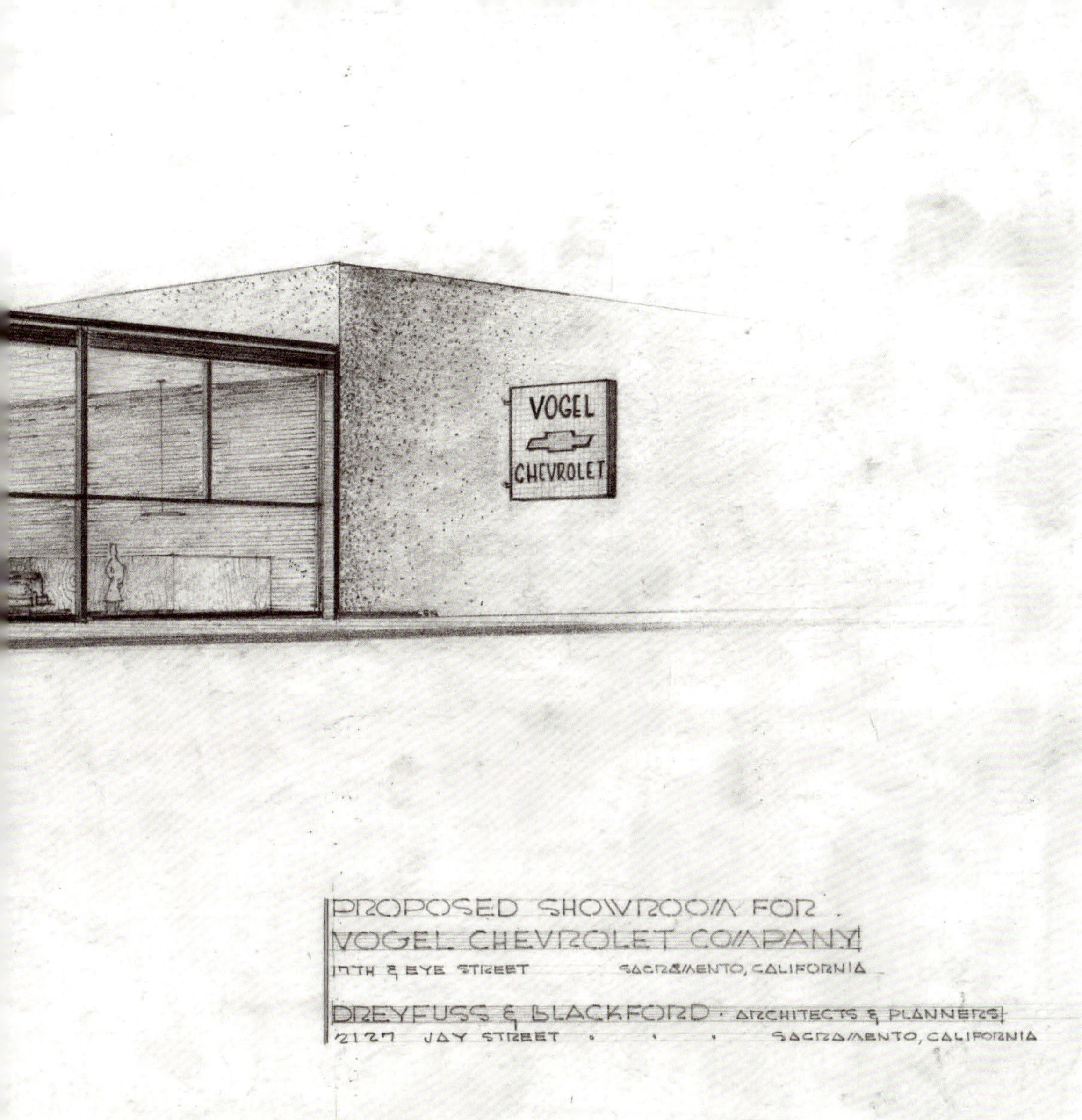

VOGEL
CHEVROLET

PROPOSED SHOWROOM FOR
VOGEL CHEVROLET COMPANY
17TH & EYE STREET SACRAMENTO, CALIFORNIA
DREYFUSS & BLACKFORD · ARCHITECTS & PLANNERS
2127 JAY STREET · · · SACRAMENTO, CALIFORNIA

Vogel Chevrolet Showroom
Sacramento, California, 1959

A groundbreaking modern building in downtown Sacramento, the Vogel Chevrolet Showroom was constructed as an addition to an existing warehouse building on a limited site. The building included both a 4,500-square-foot sales showroom on the ground floor and 1,350-square-foot offices on the mezzanine.

IBM

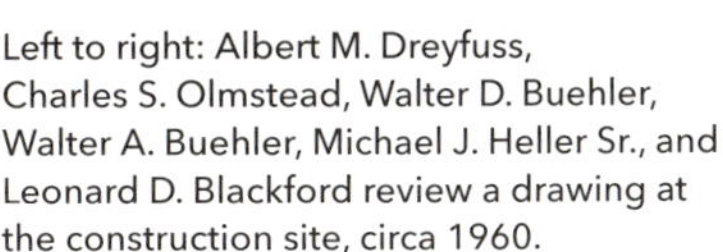

Left to right: Albert M. Dreyfuss, Charles S. Olmstead, Walter D. Buehler, Walter A. Buehler, Michael J. Heller Sr., and Leonard D. Blackford review a drawing at the construction site, circa 1960.

A rendering showing the original design with additional floors.

IBM Office Building
Sacramento, California, 1963

Winner of the Governor's Design Award in 1966, this building housed IBM's regional offices until 1992. It was one of the first precast concrete structures in Northern California and employed many innovative passive solar features. The quality and durability of the building's materials, design, and detailing ensured that it remained a viable, economical office complex for many years.

In 1964, Dreyfuss received a call from James Kennedy Carr, the new director at San Francisco International Airport (SFO). Fifteen years earlier, Carr was SMUD's assistant general manager. He paired Dreyfuss & Blackford with John Carl Warnecke and entrusted them with creating the master plan for the expansion of SFO. This aviation work led to a Dreyfuss & Blackford satellite office in San Francisco. To manage the work, the partners divided their time between Sacramento and San Francisco from 1965 to 1970. SFO's circular roadways, central garage, and curved terminals are the legacy of Blackford's planning vision. Blackford also designed for a connection to a rapid transit station, which arrived more than twenty years after his aspiration.

SNACK BAR
6
6a

San Francisco International Airport (SFO) Expansion
San Francisco, California, 1981

Dreyfuss & Blackford Architects was involved in the expansion of the San Francisco International Airport (SFO) from 1964 to 1981. The firm was responsible for a comprehensive masterplan. The first phase of its design work included the north terminal, entrance roads and terminal roads, a ground transportation center, the remodel and enlargement of the south and east terminals, and replacement of loading areas. A second phase included constructing elevated roadways and a five-story parking garage.

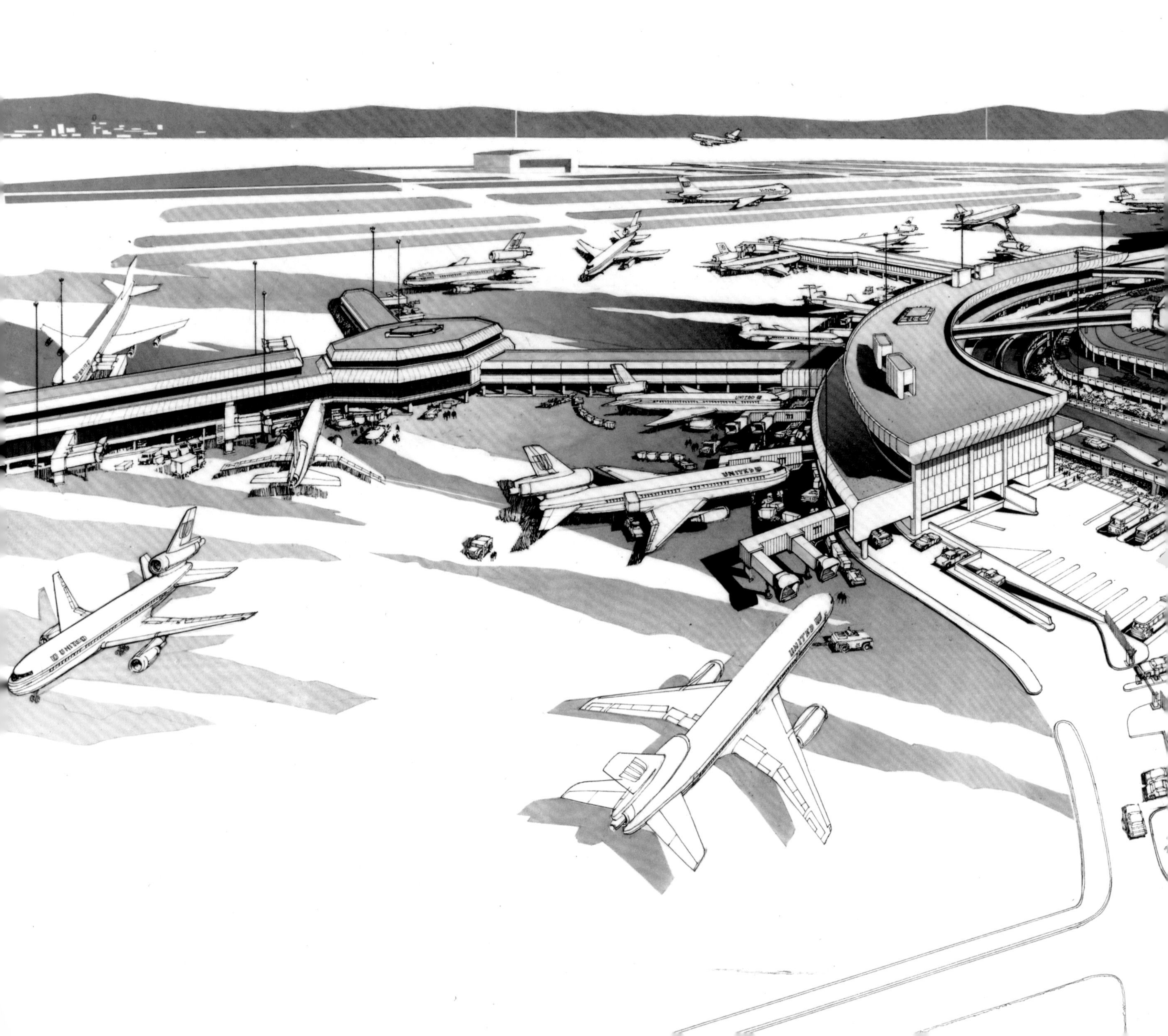
UNITED
UNITED
UNITED

As the twentieth century moved on, Dreyfuss & Blackford continued to develop projects of great importance to Northern California, such as CalPERS Headquarters Lincoln Plaza North (1987). This significant design effort effectively merged established ideas about modernism and urban design with new advances in sustainability.

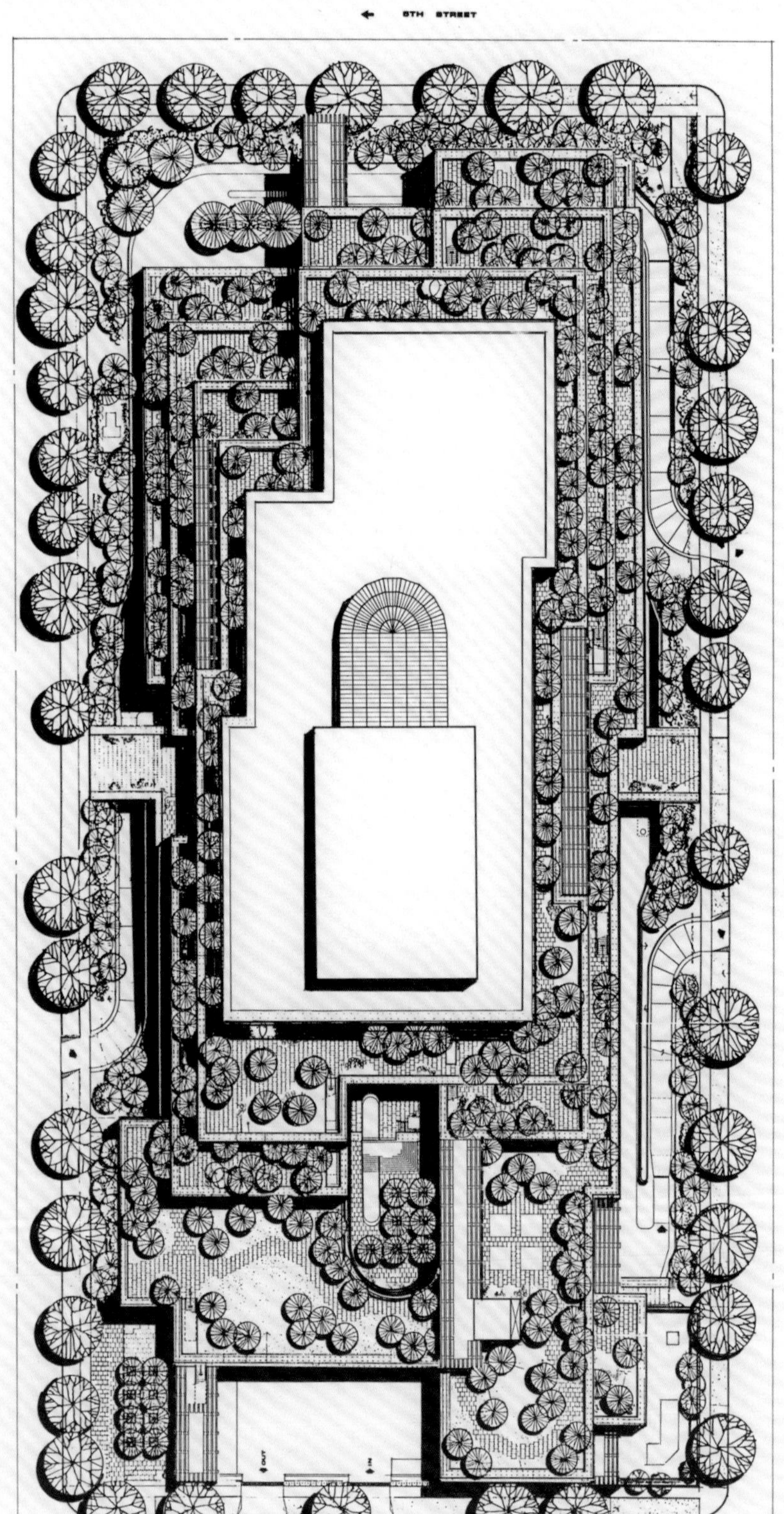
6TH STREET
P STREET
Q STREET
3RD STREET
0′
50′
100′
NORTH

Overleaf: Vegetation provides an ever-changing facade to the building.

CalPERS Headquarters Lincoln Plaza North

Sacramento, California, 1987

In the 1980s, CalPERS (California Public Employees' Retirement System) purchased land spanning two full city blocks for a new headquarters building in downtown Sacramento. Some twenty-five years after completing the SMUD Headquarters, Dreyfuss & Blackford found an opportunity to fully integrate building and landscape in the CalPERS Headquarters Lincoln Plaza North. Where SMUD was designed as a building in a park, CalPERS Headquarters was a building as a park, with lushly terraced grounds and tall interior atrium. CalPERS Headquarters—featuring raised computer floors, indirect lighting, and fully automated mechanical lighting and security controls—is one of the most technically advanced office buildings in California. It was an instant landmark when it opened in 1987. Though it is one of the largest buildings in downtown Sacramento, its size is masked by stepped landscape terraces that complement the scale of the surrounding community.

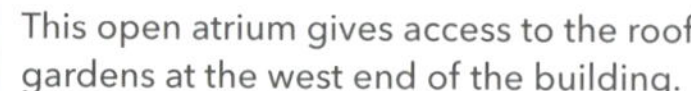

This open atrium gives access to the roof gardens at the west end of the building.

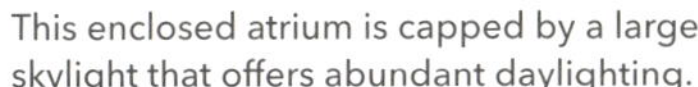

This enclosed atrium is capped by a large skylight that offers abundant daylighting.

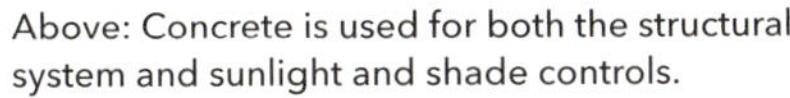

Above: Concrete is used for both the structural system and sunlight and shade controls.

Far right: Visual screening is achieved through a collaboration with artist Gordon Huether.

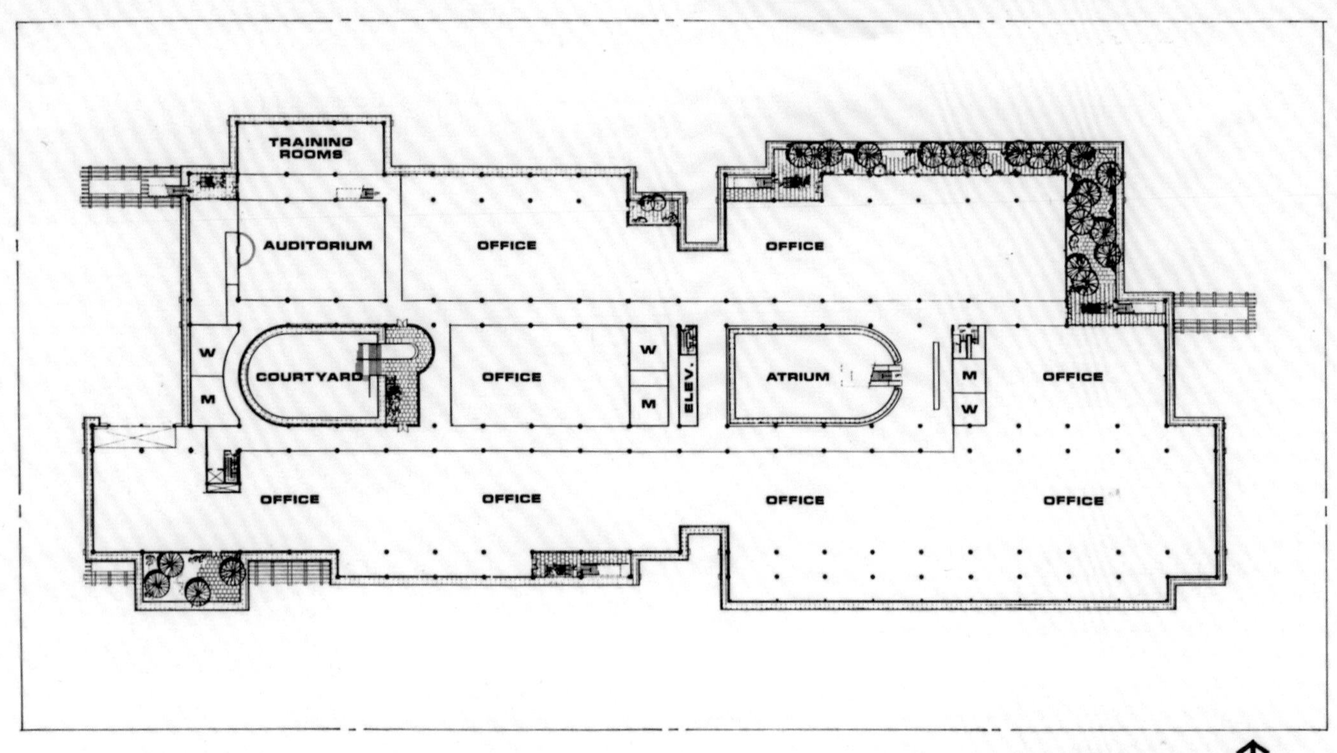

SECOND FLOOR PLAN

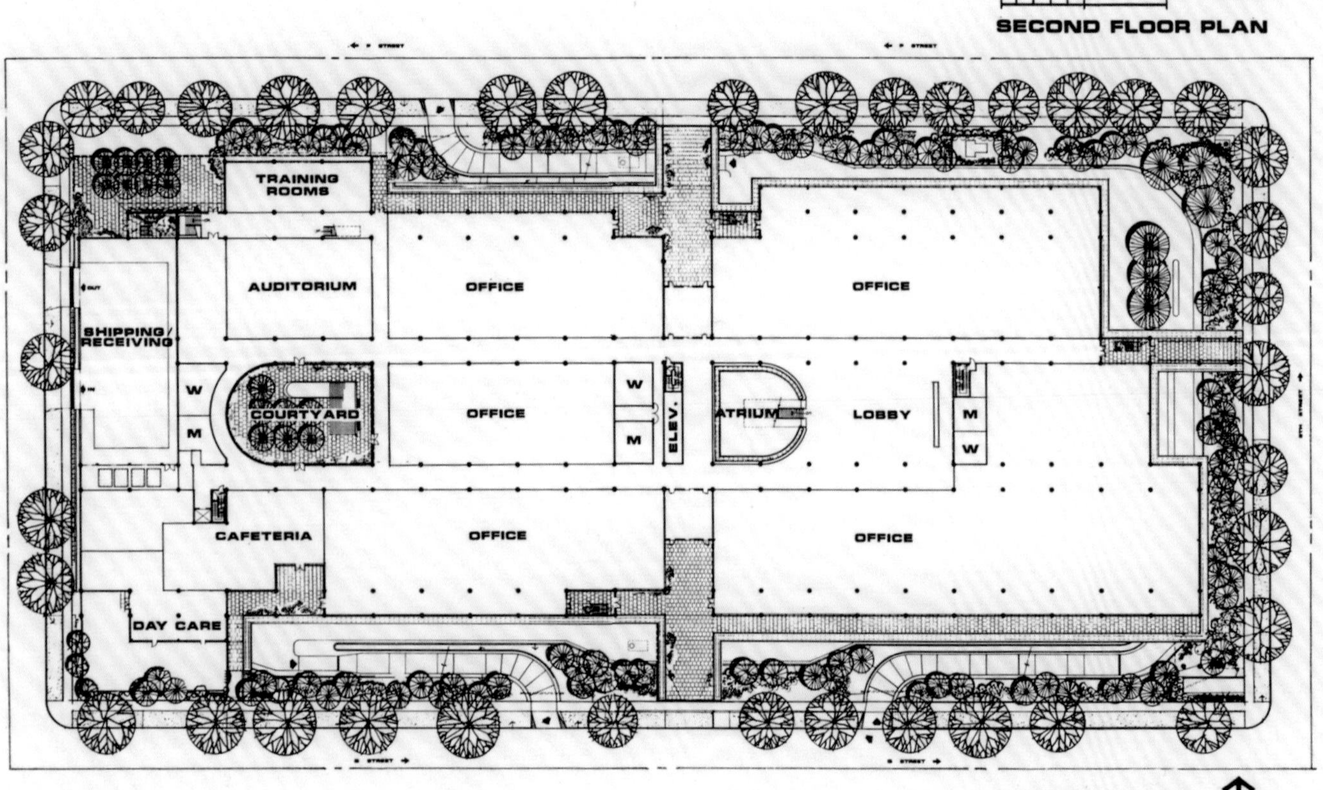

GROUND FLOOR PLAN

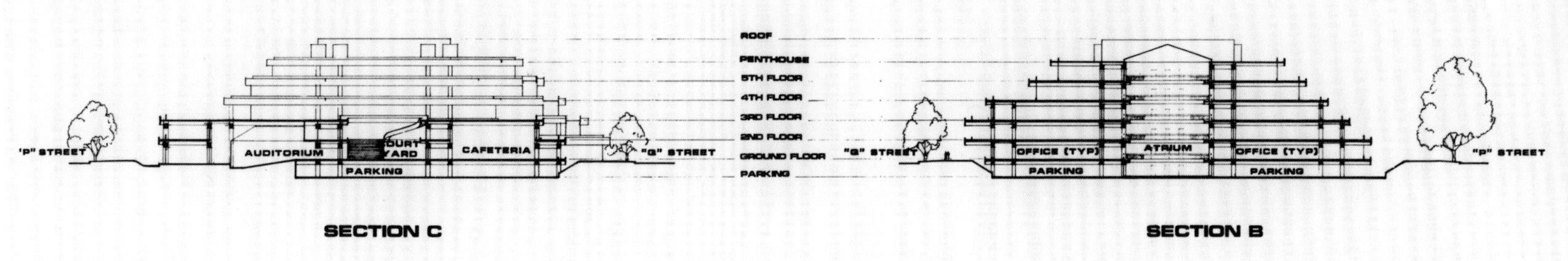
ROOF
PENTHOUSE
5TH FLOOR
4TH FLOOR
3RD FLOOR
2ND FLOOR
GROUND FLOOR
PARKING
"P" STREET
AUDITORIUM
COURT YARD
CAFETERIA
PARKING
"G" STREET
SECTION C
"G" STREET
OFFICE (TYP)
ATRIUM
OFFICE (TYP)
PARKING
PARKING
"P" STREET
SECTION B

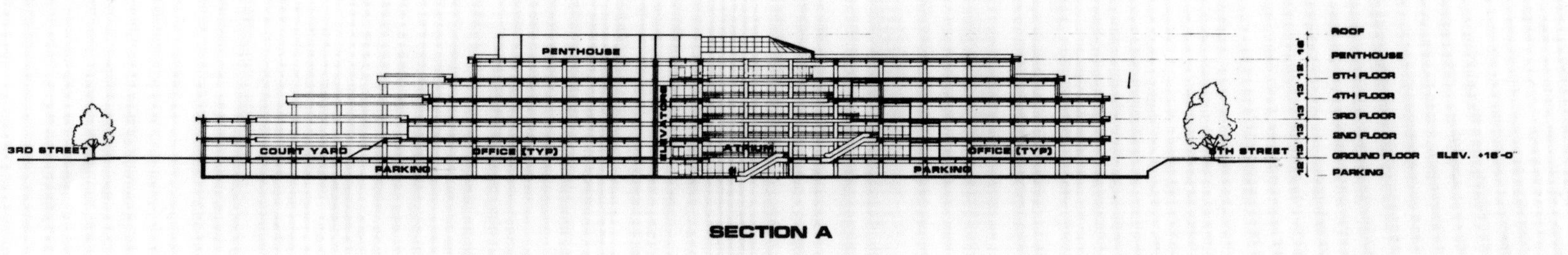
3RD STREET
COURT YARD
PARKING
OFFICE (TYP)
PENTHOUSE
ELEVATORS
ATRIUM
OFFICE (TYP)
PARKING
ROOF
PENTHOUSE
5TH FLOOR
4TH FLOOR
3RD FLOOR
2ND FLOOR
GROUND FLOOR
ELEV.
PARKING
SECTION A

In 1987, as the CalPERS Headquarters neared completion, John C. Webre joined Dreyfuss & Blackford Architects and soon became an important part of its leadership team. As the twentieth century came nearer to conclusion, both Dreyfuss and Blackford began to transition away from active involvement with their firm. The completion of their final major project, the Sacramento International Airport (SMF), Terminal A (1998), provided the right moment for the two founding partners to transition to retirement, leaving Webre to guide the firm.

Terminal A (foreground) includes extensive skylighting, notably at its large central area.

Sacramento International Airport (SMF), Terminal A
Sacramento, California, 1998

Originally designed in the late 1980s by Dreyfuss & Blackford as a significant expansion to the existing Sacramento International Airport, Terminal A was restarted in 1995 with an update to the design. The project includes a consolidated remote rental car facility—the first of its kind in the United States. In 2004 Dreyfuss & Blackford added a new parking structure to SMF; it was the third largest in California at the time.

Baggage claim area with *Samson* installation by artist Brian Goggin.

AMERICA WEST

As the firm moved into the twenty-first century, its relationship with Sacramento State grew stronger. Building upon its Sacramento State College Master Plan (1965) with the Napa Hall College of Continuing Education Building (2003), the firm completed many significant projects for Sacramento State. Perhaps the most significant of these is the Sacramento State Academic Information Resources Center (2007). In addition to being an essential component of the core of the campus, this 100,000-square-foot, four-story, flexible data center and information and technology building has proven to be thoughtfully designed for future technology. It is as functional and well utilized today as when it opened.

Some of the firm's other notable twenty-first-century projects are the State of California Office of Emergency Services (2001), California ISO Headquarters and Operations Center (2011), and Pacific Gas and Electric Company Gas Safety Academy (2017), presented in this section. Additional recent works are featured in the Projects chapter of this book.

In 2017 Dreyfuss + Blackford Architecture opened a San Francisco office to expand its reach of potential clients. Today the firm is led by partners Kristopher Barkley, Gus Fischer, Jason A. Silva, and Scott Shannon along with John C. Webre acting as business development principal and CEO.

The building connects to the campus with multiple entrances.

California State University, Sacramento
Academic Information Resources Center
Sacramento, California, 2007

This structure draws its details and forms from existing campus buildings. At the same time, it expresses new technology and provides a comfortable amenity for students. Its material palette of aluminum, zinc, and lightweight precast concrete panels brings a new level of quality to the campus.

GAS SAFETY AC

Pacific Gas and Electric Company (PG&E) Gas Safety Academy
Winters, California, 2017

Following a 2010 gas pipeline explosion in San Bruno, California, PG&E took measures to improve its technical training system and began planning for a new, consolidated training facility. This facility effectively combines several state-of-the-art training programs at a single site. The site planning design creates clear and simple connections between components and defines outdoor areas for gatherings and informal classrooms.

Dreyfuss + Blackford Architecture Today

International Style modernism laid the foundation for Dreyfuss + Blackford Architecture as a visionary practice. Since its early years, the firm has developed stylistically, yet it continues to design projects of great significance and lasting value. This book provides a window into the continuing desire to improve our practice and design projects that honor the legacy of Albert M. Dreyfuss and Leonard D. Blackford.

Though designed to be utilitarian and economical, the building has colorful elements that provide warmth and interest.

Practice

Dreyfuss + Blackford Architecture has a long history of designing large, complex projects with distinct programs. The firm enjoys working on diverse building types and engaging with new and innovative collaborators. To achieve transformative success in a project and provide the highest level of human-centered design excellence, we strive to build understanding and alignment with our project's owners, its users, and the community it affects.

We realize success for our work through practices that develop strong team alignment. The processes and exercises discussed in this chapter represent a firm-wide culture that engages with people to achieve the strongest outcomes.

Notes from our initial workflow process sessions.

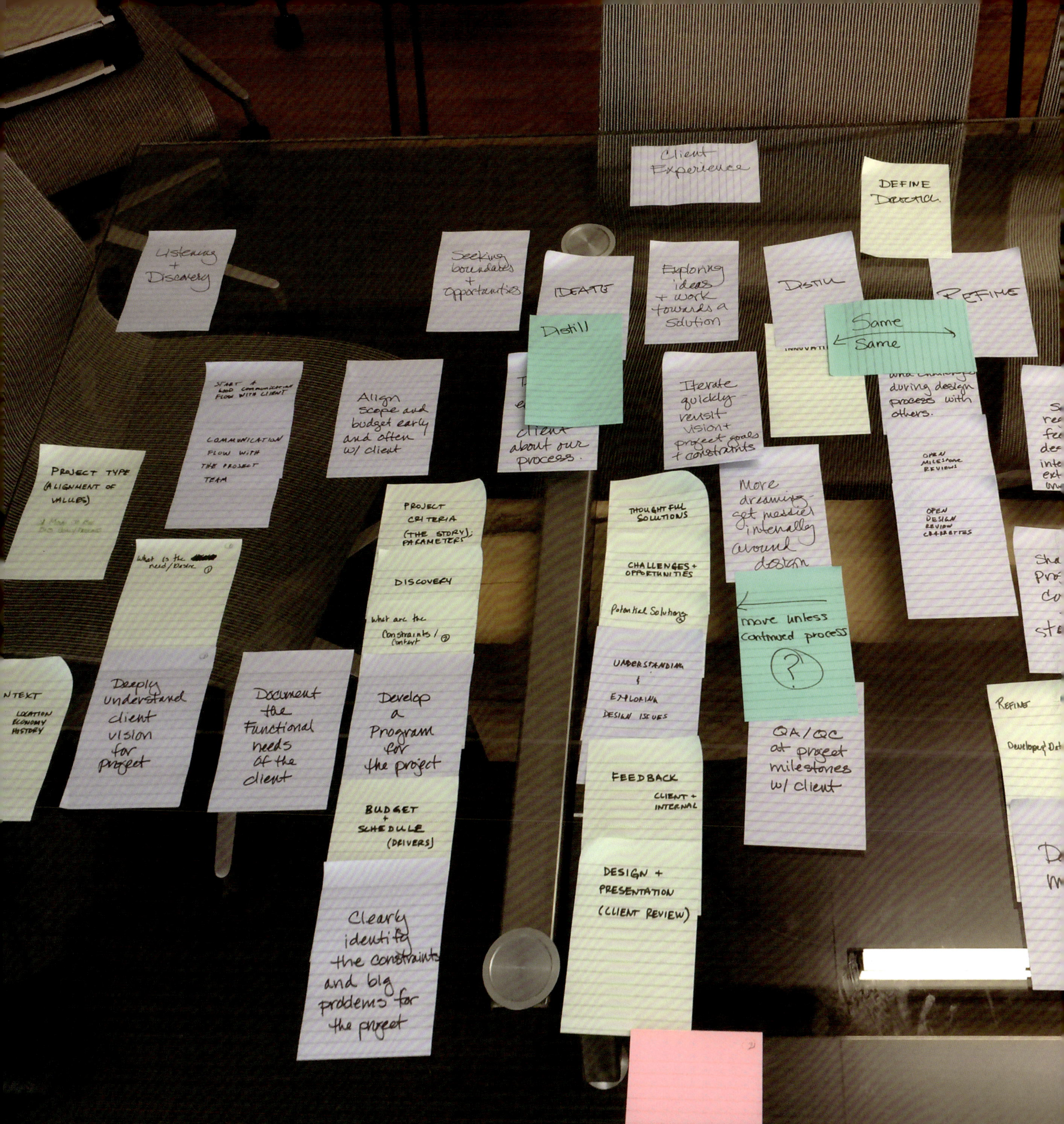

Client Experience
DEFINE DIRECTION
Listening + Discovery
Seeking boundaries + opportunities
IDEATE
Distill
Exploring ideas + work towards a solution
DISTILL
REFINE
Same
Same
Align scope and budget early and often w/ client
client about our process.
Iterate quickly - revisit vision + project goals + constraints
during design process with others.
PROJECT TYPE (ALIGNMENT OF VALUES)
COMMUNICATION FLOW WITH THE PROJECT TEAM
PROJECT CRITERIA (THE STORY); PARAMETERS
DISCOVERY
What are the Constraints / Context
More dreaming - get messier internally around design
OPEN MILESTONE REVIEWS
OPEN DESIGN REVIEW CHARRETTES
THOUGHTFUL SOLUTIONS
CHALLENGES + OPPORTUNITIES
Potential Solutions
move unless continued process
?
UNDERSTANDING + EXPLORING DESIGN ISSUES
LOCATION ECONOMY HISTORY
Deeply understand client vision for project
Document the Functional needs of the client
Develop a Program for the project
BUDGET + SCHEDULE (DRIVERS)
QA/QC at project milestones w/ client
FEEDBACK CLIENT + INTERNAL
DESIGN + PRESENTATION (CLIENT REVIEW)
Clearly identify the constraints and big problems for the project

Workflow Process Development

As Dreyfuss + Blackford Architecture shifted from serial to concurrent project delivery, we found that traditional office hierarchies did not serve the work well. We developed a firm-wide culture of inclusion and engagement centered on team-based project design. This new model connects all participants, from staff members to clients to consultants, in the project. Dreyfuss + Blackford devoted significant effort to developing new work processes that reflect our inclusive approach. The firm's leadership brought together a diverse group to generate proposals that were shared, reviewed, critiqued, and developed by a large cross-section of our staff over a long period. We continue to refine this process as projects stretch its framework with new challenges.

Design excellence can be found throughout the architecture of Dreyfuss + Blackford. While this excellence informs our identity, our team came to understand that a greater consistency in the quality of our efforts could vastly improve our projects' outcomes. Development of a defined process, or workflow, for engaging our clients, partners, and staff facilitates this desired consistency and allows for the successes of the past to better inform our current work.

At the core of the workflow examination is a desire to infuse our process with a thoughtful approach to both the design and technical aspects of our projects. Dreyfuss + Blackford continues to develop workflow tools to ensure that regardless of the project or the people working on it we always bring a unique and deliberate approach to our collaboration.

process

At the start of this development, we analyzed the traditional architectural project delivery phases—pre-design, schematic design, design development, construction documents, and construction administration. We came to realize that this method of organization is missing an important component, it creates order but does not intrinsically encourage better design and team dynamics. We sought to redefine this approach to include important considerations of design quality, engagement, and collaboration. Rather than use conventional names for these phases, we assigned new titles that more specifically relate to aspirational goals of encouraged exploration and innovation.

Discovery and Definition

Traditionally described as pre-design, programming, or project definition, this phase builds a solid foundation for design to begin. In this phase, we give special attention to understanding the underlying needs of the client and potentially a much larger body of related groups and individuals that might include client customers, neighbors, community groups, and regulatory agencies. These needs are folded into a definitions document that serves as the basis for design and acts as future reference when testing design work against project goals.

Inspiration and Direction

This phase is generally described as conceptual or schematic design. Exploration and ideation are the key components here. This is the moment when we thoughtfully begin to test the definitions learned in the Discovery and Definition phase. Diagramming and storytelling can be used as a means of setting a project's direction and gaining acceptance. A strong diagram can be easily understood, while a well-crafted story will be easily remembered and often repeated. The message should be simple and concise. When the team is working well together the story will be obvious and come together naturally.

Refinement and Commitment

In this phase, historically known as design development, design concepts that embody the needs and aspirations of the team at large are refined into reality. Components of the design concept are carefully reviewed and developed into resolved solutions, setting a solid framework for final detailing in the next phase. An important component of this phase is a quality assurance process that includes not only technical review, but also a critical assessment of adherence to the original design concepts. This review is not intended to be all encompassing. It focuses on details and developed design components that have a significant effect on the project's overall design quality.

Delivery and Launch

Wrapping up everything into a well-built set of construction documents is key here. This phase also serves as the last moment to assure that design intent is effectively communicated to the builder.

Stewardship and the Extraordinary

Even though construction has started, design is still a priority. There are many moments where details might change due to construction methods or general misunderstandings, and these require thinking about design continuity.

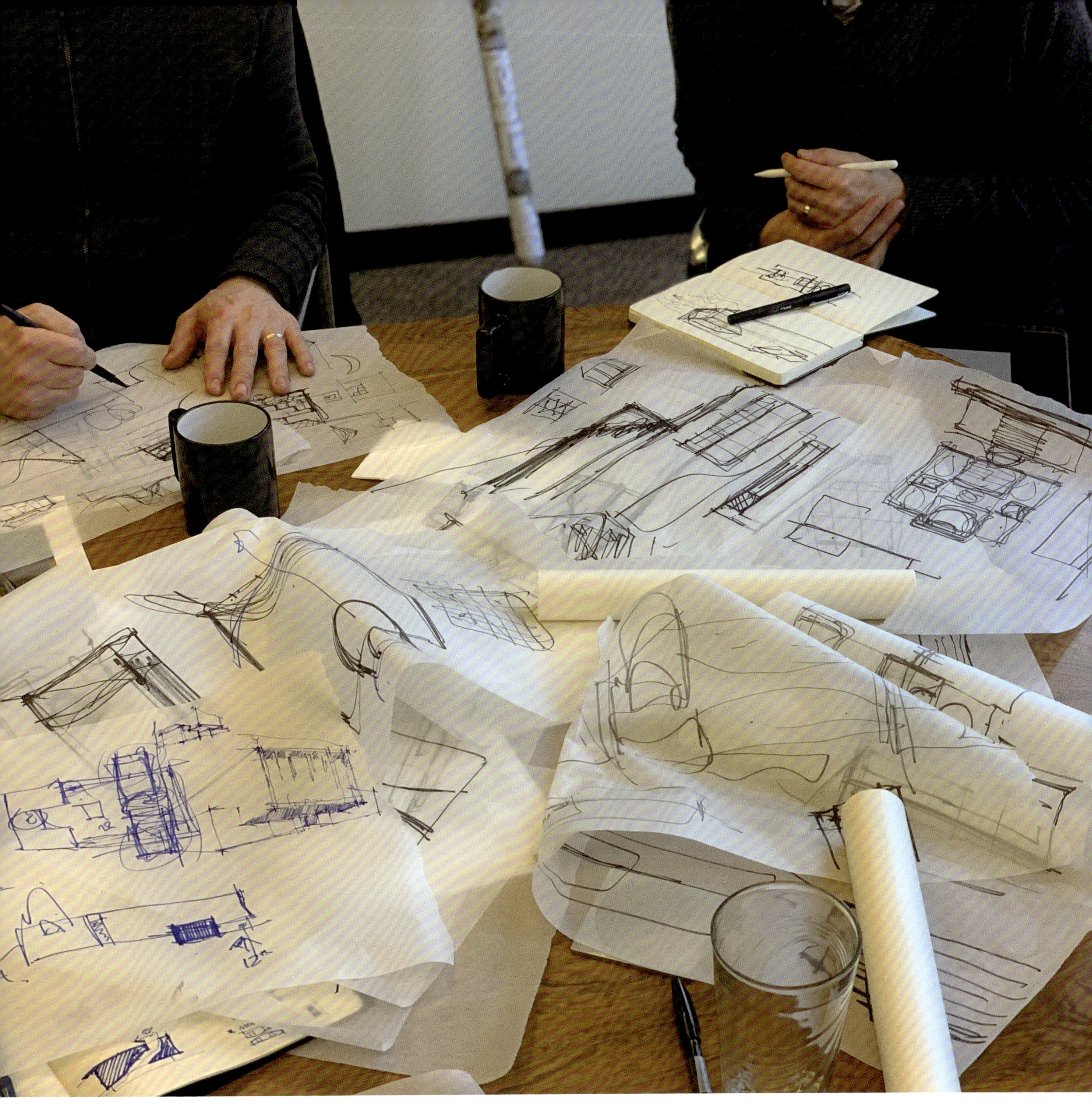

To organize the workflow within each phase, we apply a simple structure to the work within the phases. Each of these five phases is broken down into three basic components:

Input
The first component consists of information, data, and reports that have been gathered as a precursor to starting the project or as output from the previous phase.

Throughput
This component consists of the primary work for each phase. It may have up to three sub-components. Gather: this term, used mostly in the earlier phases of the project, defines the process of using outreach, open discussion, and research to build a foundation for the work to come. Cook: this term describes the work that occurs more independently from the client and provides a product that can be reviewed and tested. Distill: once the basic product has been created from the cooking process, it is refined and adjusted with client input to assure that the right solutions are brought to the Output component of the phase.

Output
This is generally found in the form of a document, drawing, or a report that serves as a deliverable for the respective phase. Ideally, this document serves as a sign-off moment before continuing to the subsequent phase.

Building a better workflow has effectively engaged a broad cross-section of Dreyfuss + Blackford in the development of quality design that is purposeful while being aspirational. The workflow process produces architecture that is built from a complete understanding of constraints and client needs while being true to our modernist roots.

INPUT
THRU-PUT
OUTPUT
REVIEW
SUPPORT

our design

Architecture at its most basic is forming space around a predetermined need. A factory is designed with the sole intent of producing a building that will produce something else. The technical brief for a factory is quantitatively defined by maximizing efficiency and production. The factory workers cannot easily be quantified, and historically their qualitative needs have often been overlooked in design briefs. If architecture aims to be successful, it must consider the people who interact with it and understand their perspectives.

This text outlines some of the processes Dreyfuss + Blackford has developed to put people at the forefront of its designs. We design environments that not only support the functional needs of every potential user but also exceed those demands. We strive to create spaces that invoke joy, excite creativity, and make lasting positive impacts on all.

Study for UC Davis Sacramento Campus Mobility Hub, 2020.

The Human Connection

The first moments of connecting and communicating with people can be the most beneficial. Working carefully through initial meetings is critical in aligning people with project goals. This consensus must be reached early—before discussing design or considering solutions. An aligned team defines what is important to each member and creates the opportunity for exceptional design solutions. When common goals are agreed upon early in the process, the design work has a strong foundation.

One example of Dreyfuss + Blackford's efforts to align the goals of a project is the UC Davis Sacramento Campus Mobility Hub (2020). We developed the project through an extensive engagement process that involved numerous interactions and workshops. During the gather phase, our team sought to discover the core issues for a transit hub for a teaching hospital. We landed on a simple proposition: that clarity—defined as "I know where I am, I know where I want to go, and I know how to get there"—was the most important and common thread for each unique user. At this point, we had no design concepts, sketches, or potential solutions, just diagrams and text to support our proposition. When we revealed the design concept of clarity, our clients immediately agreed that it did not need further explanation or change. The concept was successful because it understood and addressed people's needs.

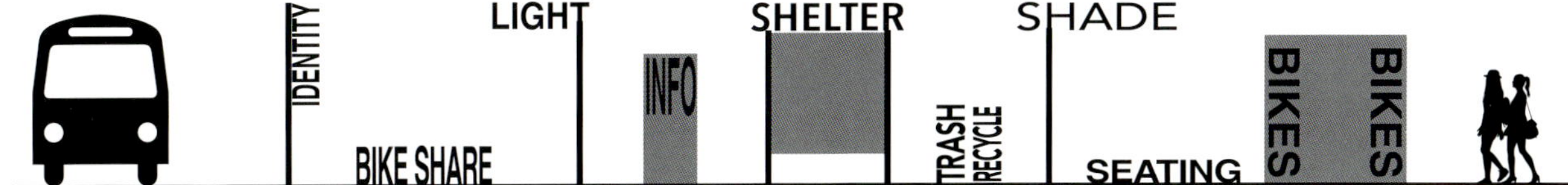

Typical transporation center evolves over time with addition of useful amenities.

Landscape growth provides valuable shade and quality of space but occludes context.

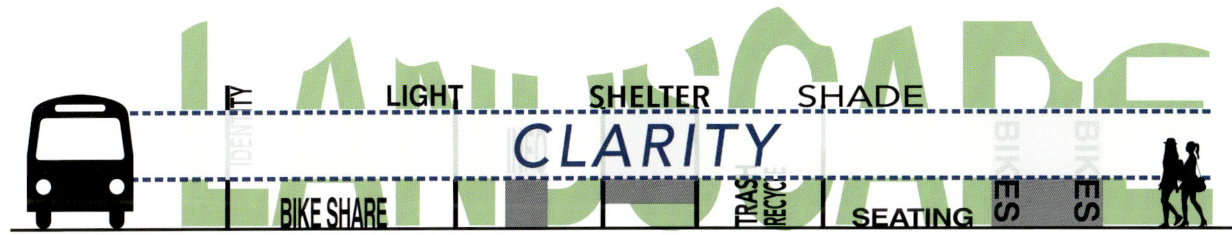

Define a zone of clear space for understanding context and clarity of place.

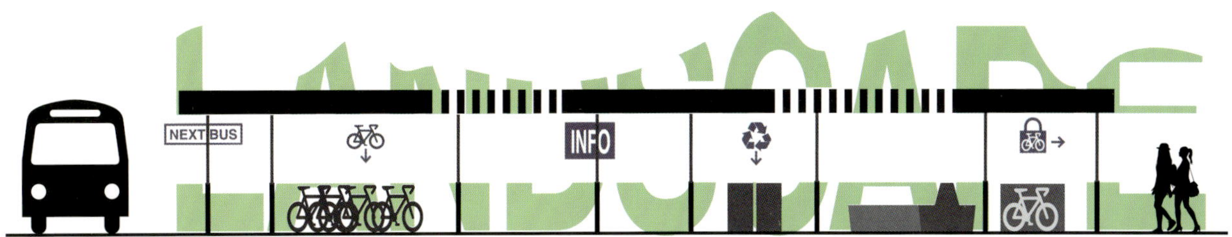

Only necessary information for the mobility hub is inside the zone of clarity.

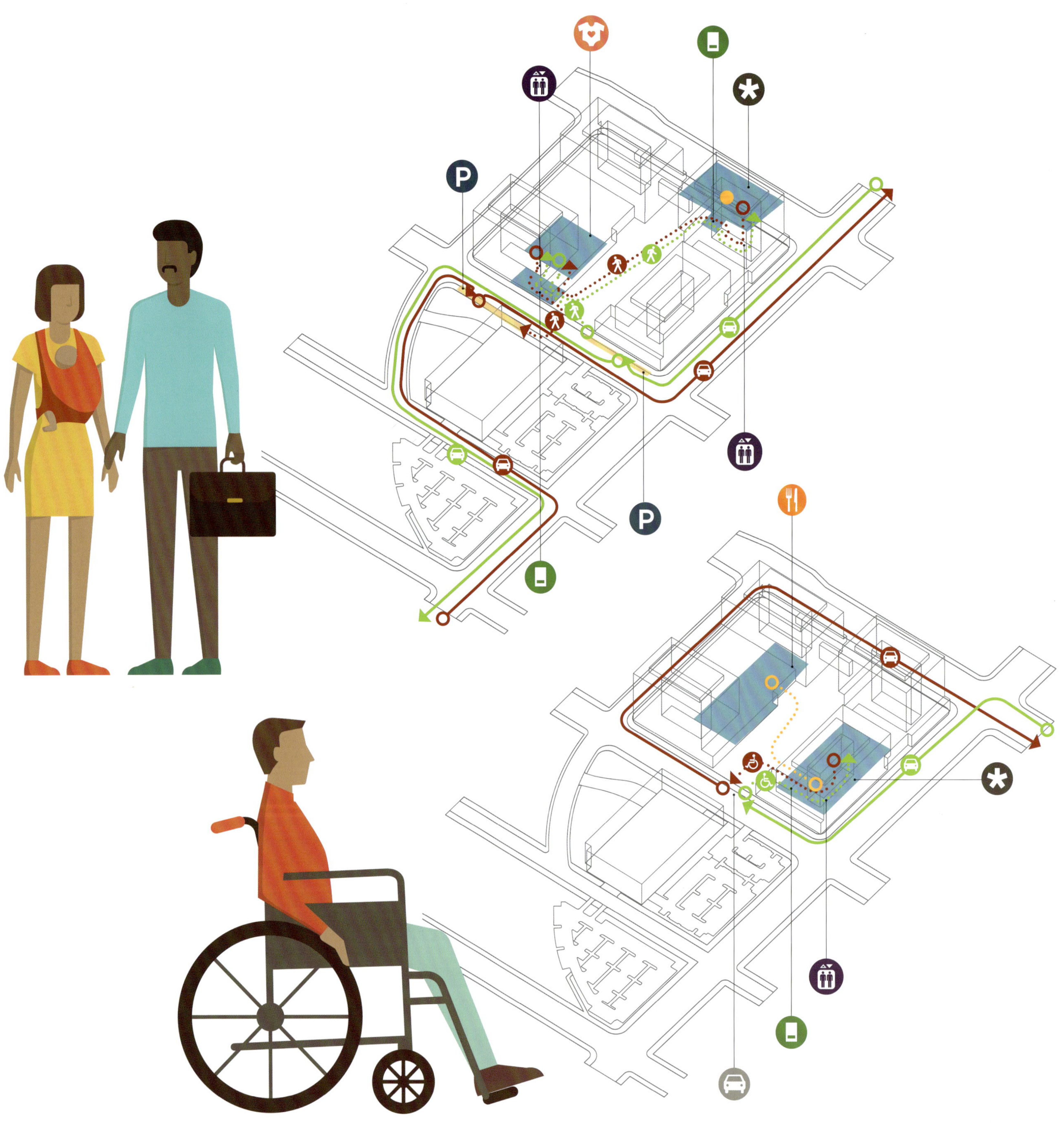

Global
Experience from the outside world.

Community Space
Experience on-approach and in shared spaces.

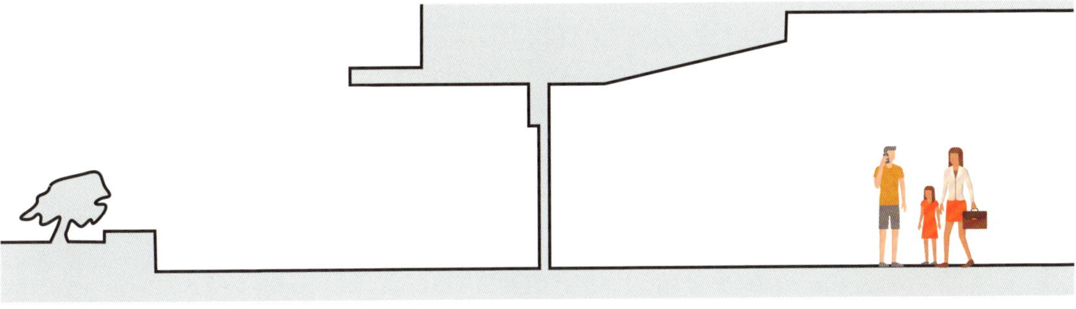

Personal Space
Experience in private spaces.

Haptic
Experience with direct physical and functional space and equipment.

Persona Mapping

During the design process, we try to disregard assumed solutions so that we can generate multiple possibilities and evaluate all of them without prejudice. This allows for greater design options. To support our focus on people, we consider a broad variety of users. This allows the design team and the project stakeholders to avoid bias in predicting users' needs. During the initial project gather phase, we and the client select personae from a library we have created. This allows us to define all the people who may be impacted by the design and to determine their needs and expectations. The better we address the concerns of each individual persona, the more successful the project.

Throughout the project, we check our design decisions against the different personae and their needs using various exercises: mapping each persona's daily routine, testing their interactions and points of potential conflict, and evaluating options through different persona's perspectives. Persona mapping is an effective way to remove the unconscious bias that a client or design team may bring to a familiar project.

Experimentation

Our team exercises its creativity to maintain the potential for high-quality work, and this requires the freedom to experiment. The results of our work as architects are typically static, built spaces. We evaluate designs through words and visual tools that can offer only approximations of the potential outcome. Successful solutions typically depend on architects' expertise in developing projects of similar scope. But what if we could experiment with designs in full-scale?

Inexpensive and easily formed materials combined with a space to build without limits provided for creative experimentation. Working with a team of artists, Dreyfuss + Blackford staff, architecture students and many volunteers, we constructed large temporary pavilions that offered an opportunity for design exploration. One of the pavilions experimented with nesting and telescoping triangular corrugated cardboard forms. We then assembled hundreds of similar tubes to form a pavilion for the 2013 LAUNCH Festival in downtown Sacramento.

Cardboard and felt walls in the innovation lab at VSP Vision Care.

We later adopted the pavilion's form and material in the flexible walls in The Shop @ VSP Global (2014). Dreyfuss + Blackford worked with members of the Hacker Lab, a maker space in Sacramento, to conceptualize, form, and test a new innovation lab for VSP Vision Care, a not-for-profit company.

The Shop was moving into the former Vogel Chevrolet Showroom in Sacramento. Dreyfuss + Blackford designed this modern glass box building in 1956, and it had undergone many uses since then. It would become a think-tank and prototyping lab for VSP. The Shop used the triangular cardboard columns first designed for temporary structures for the LAUNCH Festival pavilion. The result of the effort at The Shop was a space that was flexible, buildable, and breakable, and ultimately part of an experiment from which many people have learned.

Understanding People's Needs

Working openly with the public, down to the grass-roots community level, can inform the design of even the largest projects. It can be a significant challenge to gain a community's trust and to have it accept architecture that may seem antithetical to its interests. By directly involving local people in the generation of a design, Dreyfuss + Blackford taps into their imagination and gains their trust.

The design combines a series of large vertical fins that are cut into a windblown form, inspired by the high winds that are common to the region. Community-generated design is part of these fins. A cycle of brightly colored canvases—painted by local families during a festival event—are abstracted in an LED light display on the building. The design team looks forward to children exclaiming to their parents, "That's my painting!" while riding down the highway.

The scheme for the Fairfield Transportation Center is an example of community-generated design. The design team knew that, despite commuters' interest in supporting sustainable park-and-ride options, it would be a challenge to gain community support for a parking structure. We worked with the City of Fairfield to help people realize the potential of an iconic landmark along the freeway. Roughly halfway between San Francisco and Sacramento, Fairfield goes unnoticed among the continuum of suburban communities. Its residents were interested in building something remarkable that would set it apart.

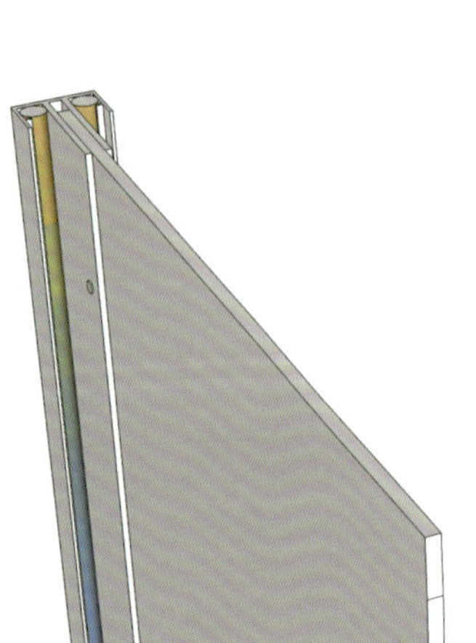

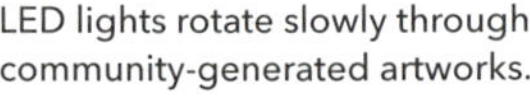

LED lights rotate slowly through community-generated artworks.

Infrastructural architecture need not be simply decorated or obfuscated when there is potential to create space that improves people's lives. We were challenged to locate a seven-story parking structure at the main entrance of the UC Davis Health Hospital in Sacramento (2010). Our design needed to maintain an open and daylit parking experience while blocking views into patients' rooms. As the structure is at a primary street intersection, its location at the front door of the UC Davis Sacramento campus required an aesthetic and sensitive screening solution.

Daylighting inside the structure improves safety and experience.

The structure's facade is made of nearly four-thousand glossy white louvers. On the street side, the louvers angle out at the top, reflecting the activity of the street while obscuring the cars inside. The louvers that face the hospital project out at the bottom, blocking all views into the adjacent hospital tower. They are specifically patterned to diffuse the daylight that is reflected inside the structure, creating an even level of light regardless of the sun angle.

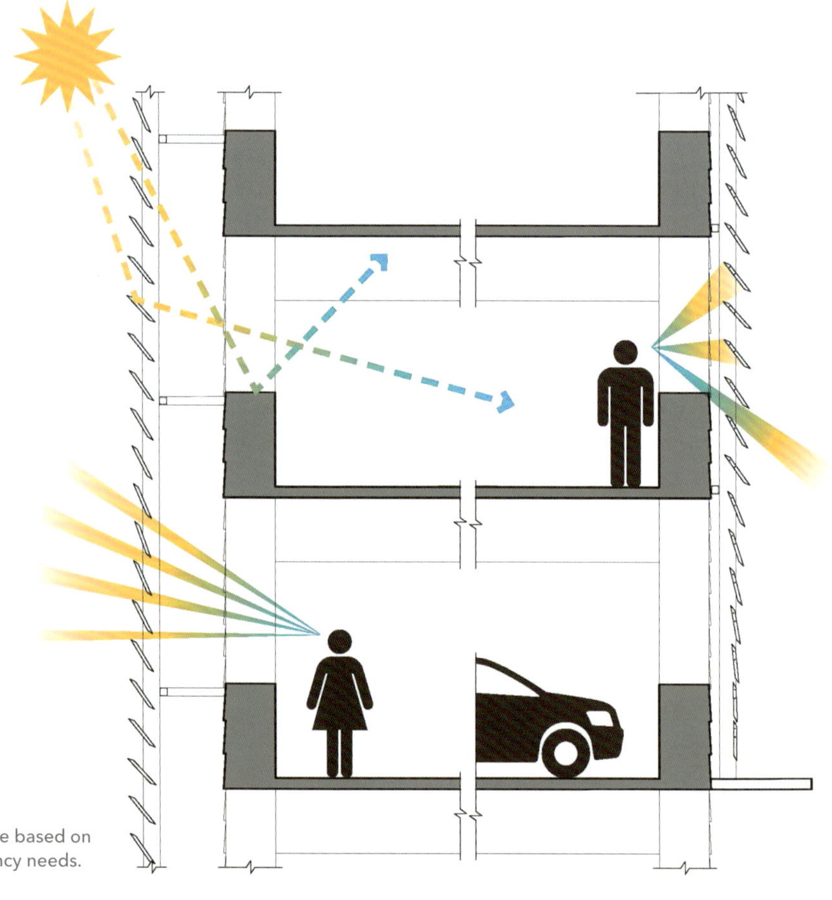

Facade louver angles are based on daylighting and adjacency needs.

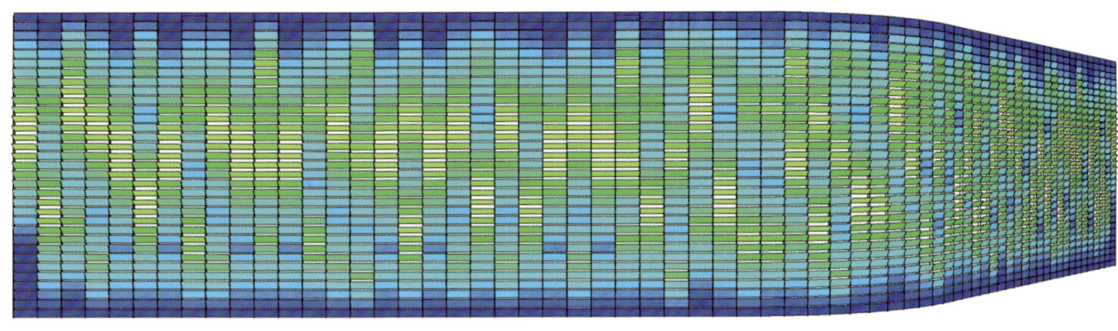

Success for Dreyfuss + Blackford is about achieving human-centered design through a rational, needs-based process. Designing for people, while seeking alignment with goals and expectations, creates high-functioning architecture that is combined with exceptional design. To that end we are constantly learning new ways, and sometimes relearning old ways, to create better spaces for people.

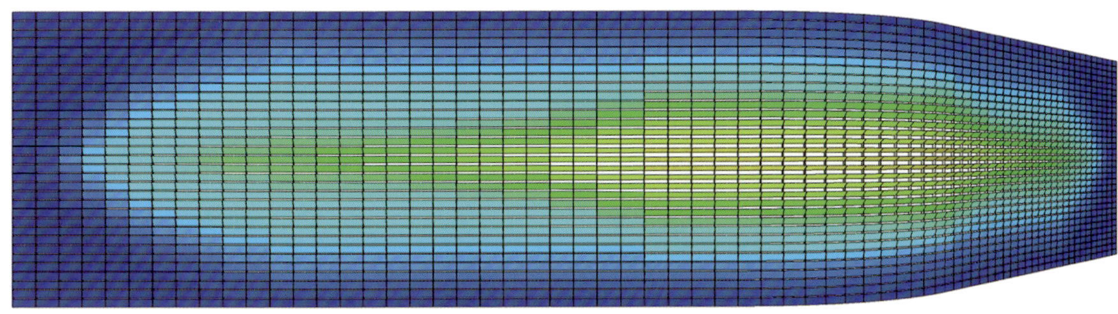

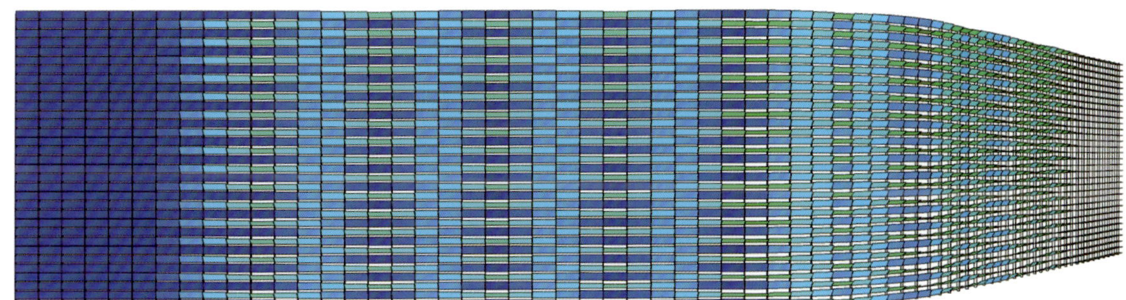

Random patterns, where yellow represents horizontal louvers and blue vertical, diffuse light throughout.

Projects

At Dreyfuss + Blackford Architecture we value our history and reputation as a firm with a broad range of expertise. This generalist approach is apparent in the diversity of our current work. The five projects featured in this chapter not only represent that diversity but also highlight our commitment to designing human-centered, sustainable, and highly functional spaces. This sample of work from the last decade illustrates the firm's connection to the values of our past and a new, fresh take on designing for the future.

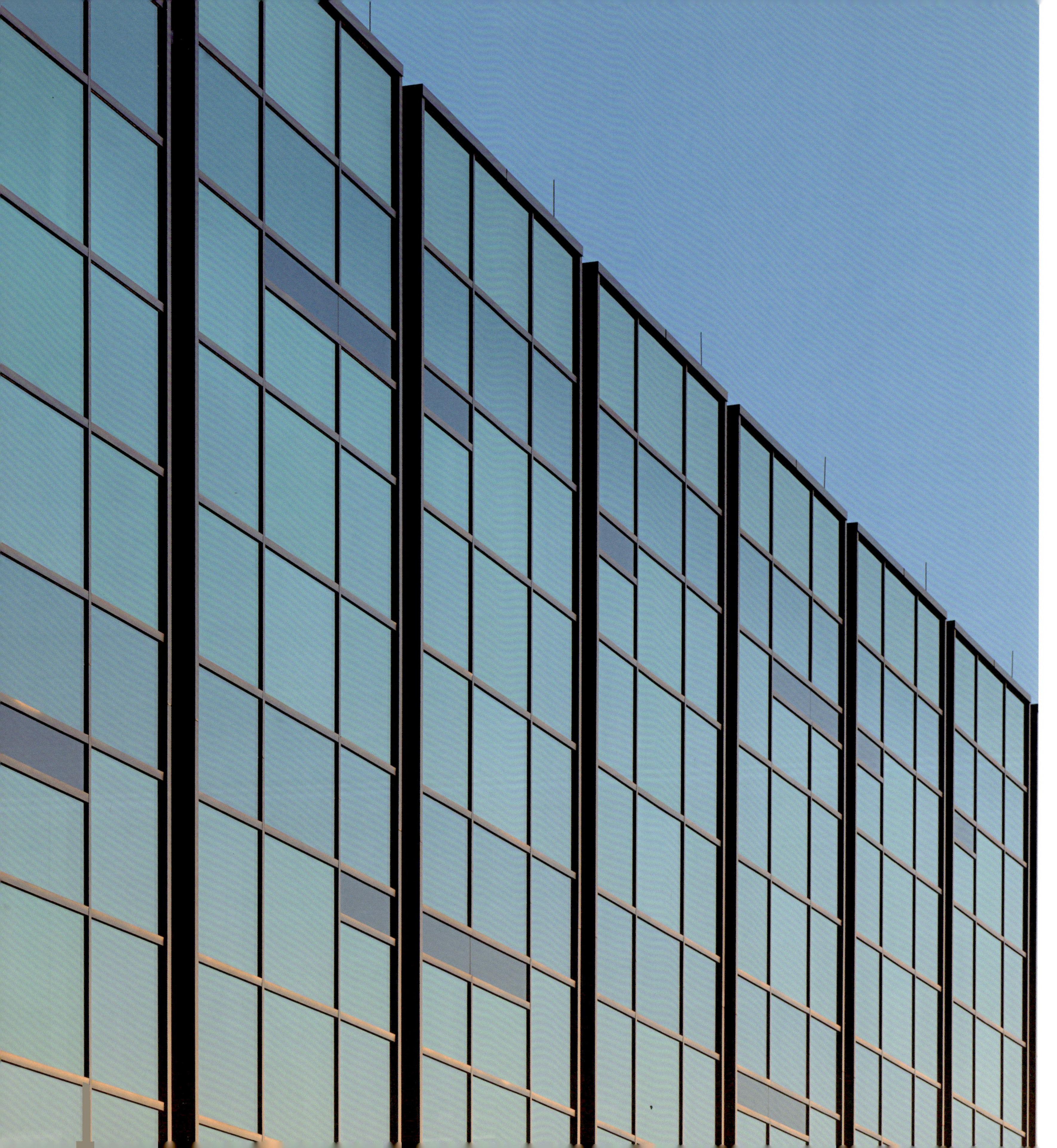

California ISO Headquarters and Operations Center

Folsom, California, 2011

The California ISO (Independent System Operator) Headquarters and Operations Center has a twenty-five-acre site of rolling grassland and native oaks in Folsom, California. Dreyfuss + Blackford developed a design with three interconnected wings specialized for three main functions. The public wing provides board and meeting rooms, training rooms, and interpretive exhibits. The multistory office wing houses staff and educational support services. The mission-critical wing provides a secure control room, data center, and electrical- and mechanical-systems plant with full system redundancy for uninterrupted operations.

The tiered building arrangement with integrated courtyard spaces allows the headquarters to follow the site contours with minimal disruption. It also provides an opportunity to direct storm water into a series of swales and detention areas that mimic the historical topography of the site. The design achieves a balance of durability and economy through intensive study of structural systems and materials. Dreyfuss + Blackford considered more than eight different building layouts to achieve the best possible functional layout while maintaining the natural feel of the site.

The office wing uses a structural precast concrete frame for durability and economy. Designed much like a loft building, this structure is easy to reconfigure and utilizes an underfloor air and data cabling system. The frame stores cool energy at night and provides a thermal lag that is beneficial during operating hours.

The mission-critical wing uses precast concrete sandwich panels with an insulating foam core. These contribute to the seismic resistance of the structure and provide hardening for security purposes as well as create a thermally efficient building. An extensive solar array on the roof of this wing provides a significant amount of electricity for operations.

Cal ISO Headquarters provides both a high level of security for the mission-critical aspects of its owner and an attractive, comfortable work environment for recruitment and retention of employees. The design aims to create a sustainable environment that preserves the nature of the site and speaks to Cal ISO's mission.

Cal ISO is a public-benefit corporation that operates the state's high-voltage electrical grid and distribution system. Its mission is to assure that continuous service is supplied while providing opportunities for energy savings through collaboration between energy providers.

In keeping with Cal ISO's mission, Dreyfuss + Blackford designed this project to meet ambitious efficiency and sustainability goals. Features include thermal energy storage, extensive incorporation of photovoltaics, and preservation of native oak woodlands. The project is certified LEED Platinum. Cal ISO has a leadership position in California's energy future, and this headquarters building reflects that leadership.

Emergency

A view showing the mission-critical wing in the foreground, the office wing behind it, and the public wing at the right.

Storm water runoff and detention systems are integrated with site features.

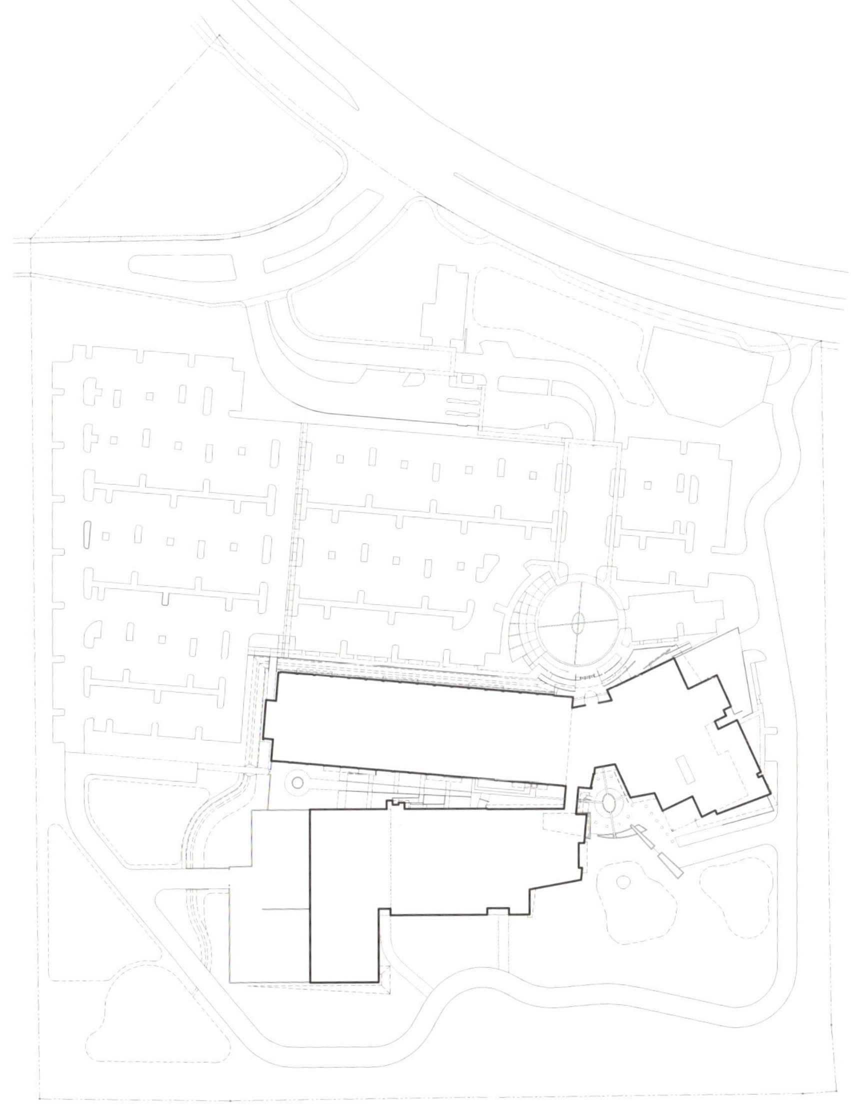

The main building entry expresses the dynamic nature of Cal ISO.

California ISO
250

A freestanding stainless steel mesh structure provides relief from direct sun.

The operations center is focused on an eighty-foot display system.

59.989
E26640

07

The office wing's central open stair connects departments and brings natural light to the core.

Open office areas benefit from the thermal mass of the exposed concrete structure and an underfloor ventilation system.

Color-coded signage wraps
corners throughout the building.

EXIT

Geared toward Cal ISO employees, this display tells the story of the project.

This space creates a transition between dining and conference areas while accommodating informal work.

EXIT

Generous outdoor space provides amenities for walking, dining, and casual meetings.

Captured space between the office and mission-critical wings offers a secure means of accessing the outdoors.

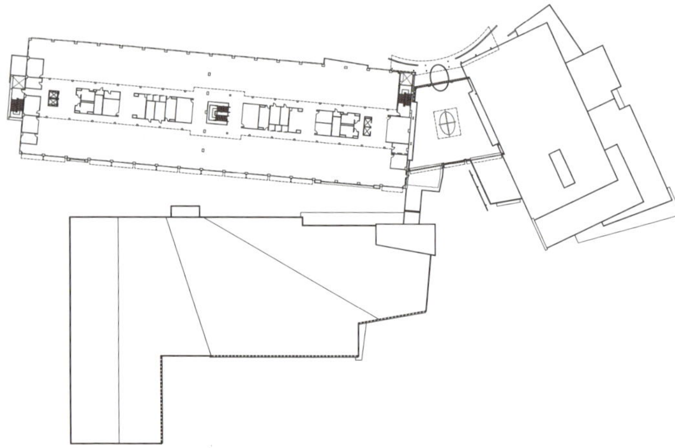
Level 2 plan.

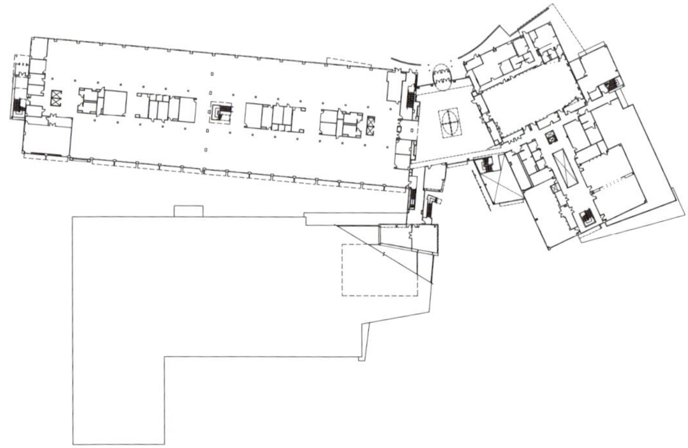
Level 1 plan.

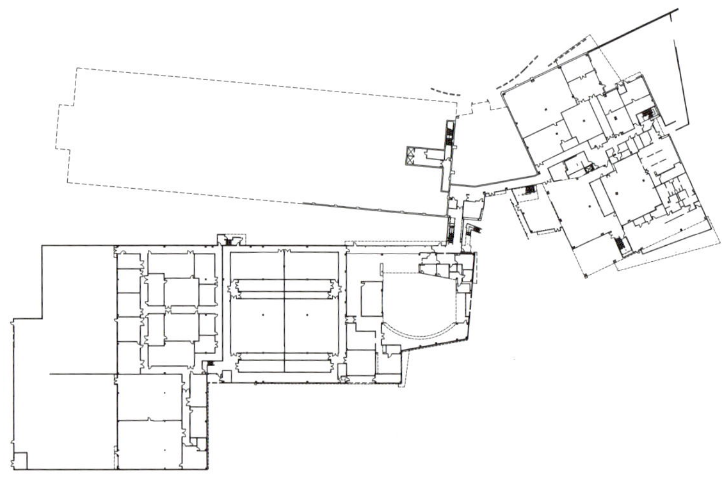
Level 0 plan.

SPEED
LIMIT
15
STOP
NO PARKING

NO PARKING FIRE LANE

VISITOR PARKING
SPEED LIMIT 15

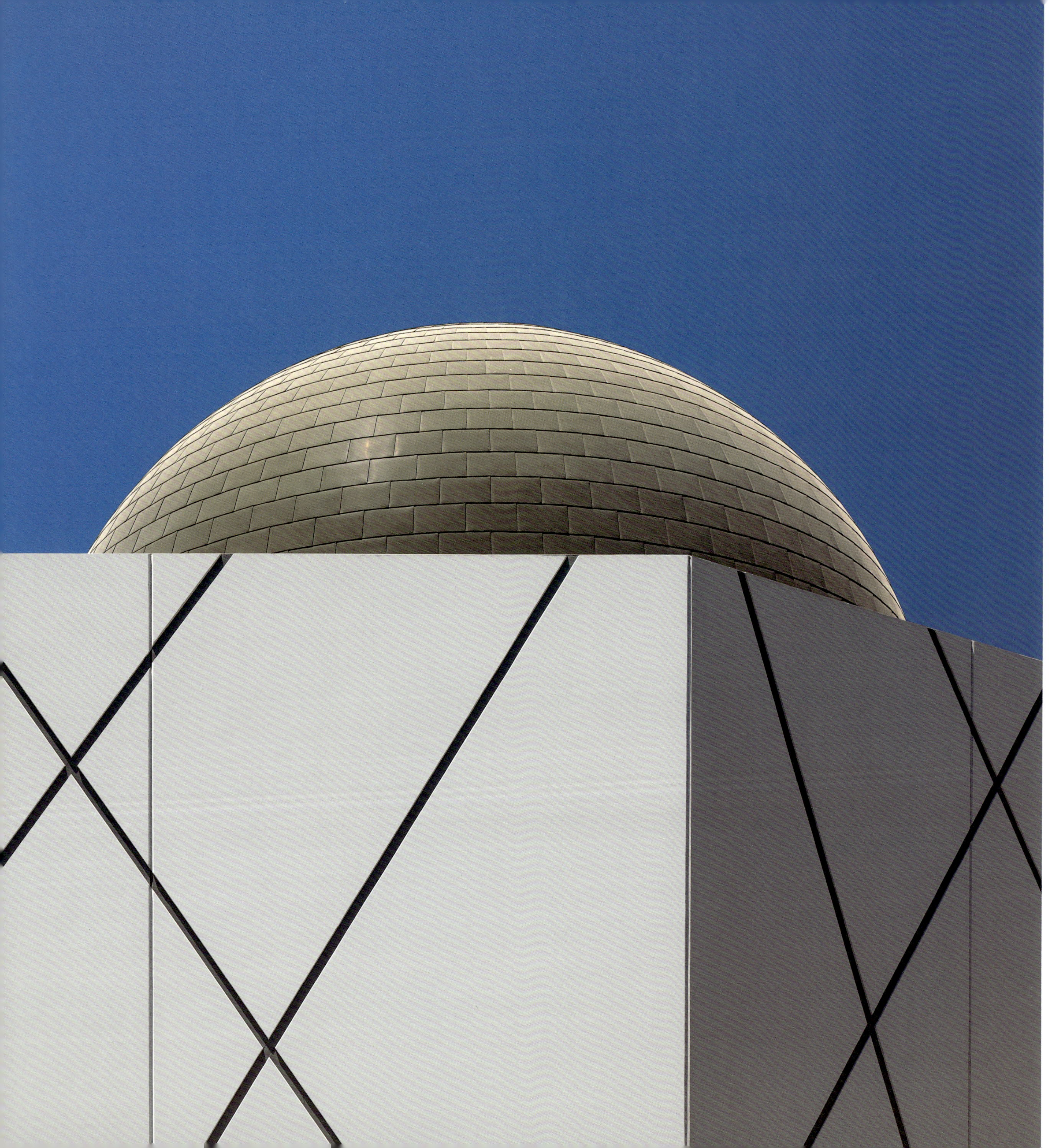

Museum of Science and Curiosity

Sacramento, California, 2021

Filling the abandoned shell of a former power station, the Museum of Science and Curiosity (MOSAC) is designed to meet MOSAC's mission of being "a dynamic epicenter for STEM education and an anchor point for Sacramento's revitalized waterfront." Inspired by the way electricity connected the local community in 1912, the science center is designed to express a similar connection to modern technology. The building's architectural expression pays respect to its history while looking to inspire the next generation of young scientists and innovators.

The historic Power Station B, designed by Willis Polk in the Beaux-Arts style in 1912, along the bank of the Sacramento River provided backup power to the Sacramento region until the 1950s. The mission of reusing the power plant was constrained by the adjacent river levee and the interstate highway, and subject to the community's desire to maintain the building's historic significance. Its boiler room and turbine room provided great volumes to accommodate MOSAC. Dreyfuss + Blackford connected a two-story addition to the east side of the original building, which allowed three well-appointed plaster reliefs on the other facades to be preserved.

In striking contrast yet in compatible scale to the historic structure, the addition comprises simple and clear volumes. One mass with a zinc-clad planetarium dome and dynamic patterned facade projects toward the highway. A simple gray color unifies various openings at its base, while a white canvas-like area is elevated to be seen by the passing traffic. This volume connects to the historic structure through an entrance cube with a distinct red glazed curtain wall. This contrasting color draws visual attention to the cube, reinforcing its use as the main entry, ticket lobby, vertical circulation, and café space.

The historic two-story power station contains exhibition spaces daylit by original steel-framed windows. The addition provides classroom space, a full-dome IMAX planetarium, a café, and offices. Open stairs feature bespoke guardrails that reflect the vector design on the facade. The café at the far side of the lobby has outdoor seating along the edge of Robert T. Matsui Waterfront Park. This park engages MOSAC with the Sacramento River and the other established cultural amenities to the south, including the California State Railroad Museum, the Crocker Art Museum, and the Old Sacramento State Historic Park. MOSAC's mission is to serve as a dynamic regional hub that engages and inspires people of all ages to explore the wonders, possibilities, and responsibilities of science. Dreyfuss + Blackford's design is intended to be a physical manifestation of that mission.

MOSAC sits along the Sacramento River, with West Sacramento beyond.

East side of Power Station B with Sacramento River beyond, circa 1912.

The addition was designed to be obscured behind the fully restored historic structure.

PACIFIC GAS AND ELECTRIC COMPANY

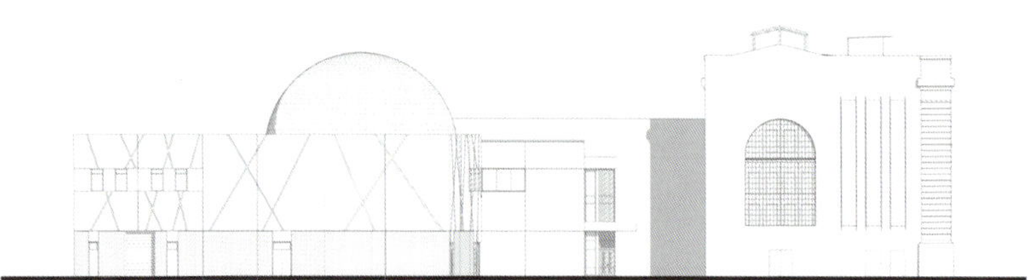
East elevation.

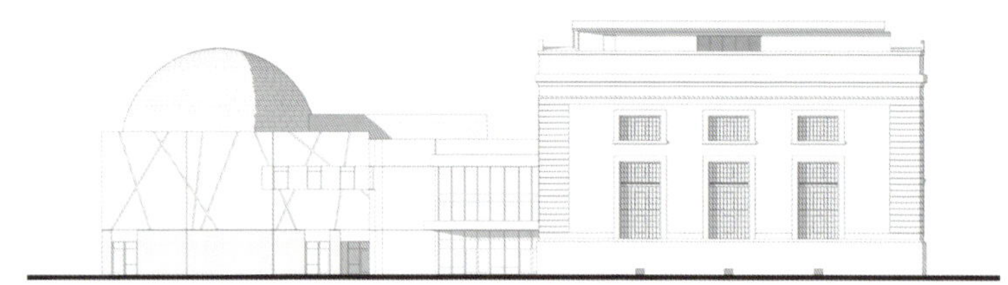
North elevation.

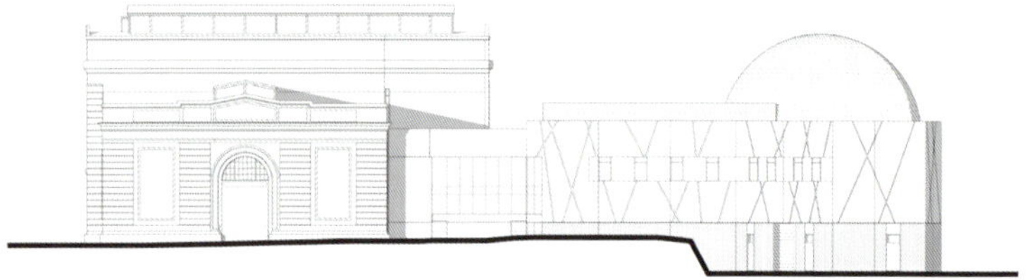
South elevation.

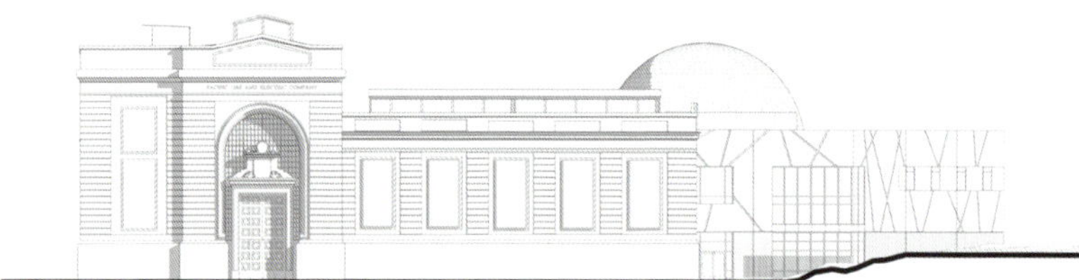
West elevation.

Bridging the new and old, a connector separates and balances the massing.

400

First floor plan.

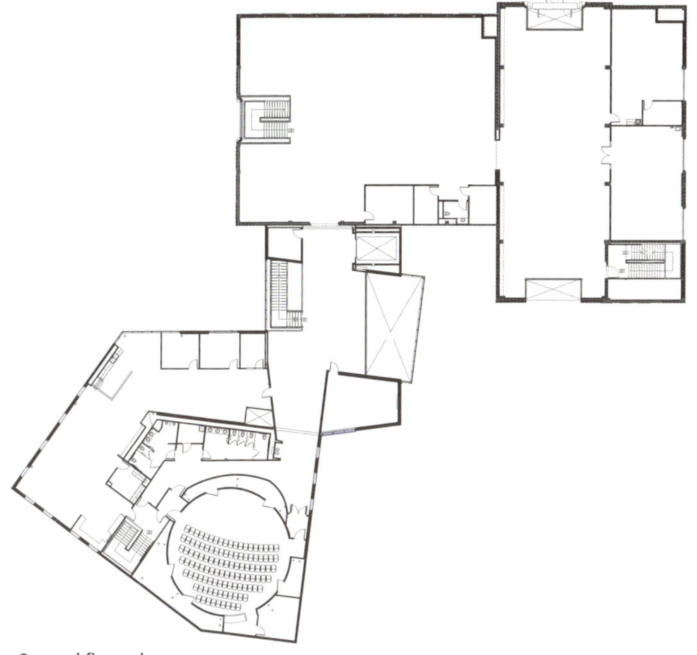
Second floor plan.

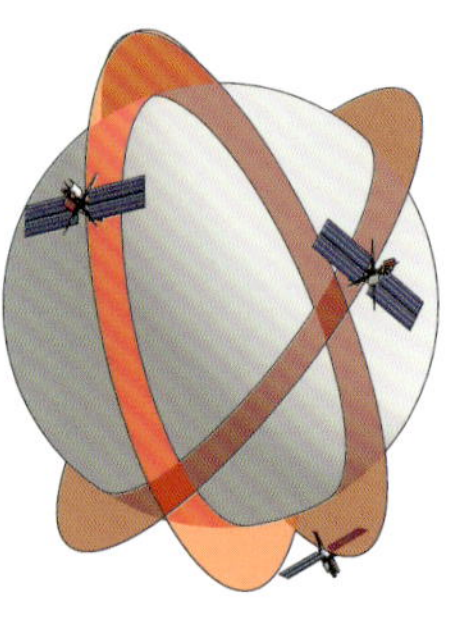
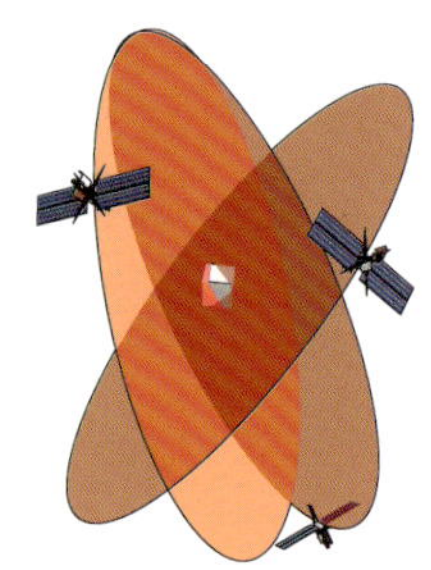
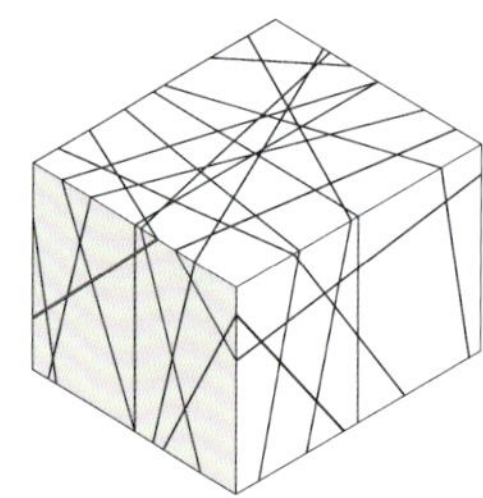

Satellite orbits inspire the facade design.

The cartouche over the entry was in a state of serious degradation, necessitating extensive reconstruction.

Monumental doors made of hardwood and clad in aluminum for resiliency replace the original doors.

BUILDING SACRAMENTO
HEALTH INNOVATIONS
Find out what's new in the world of health innovation and research in our region and around the world.

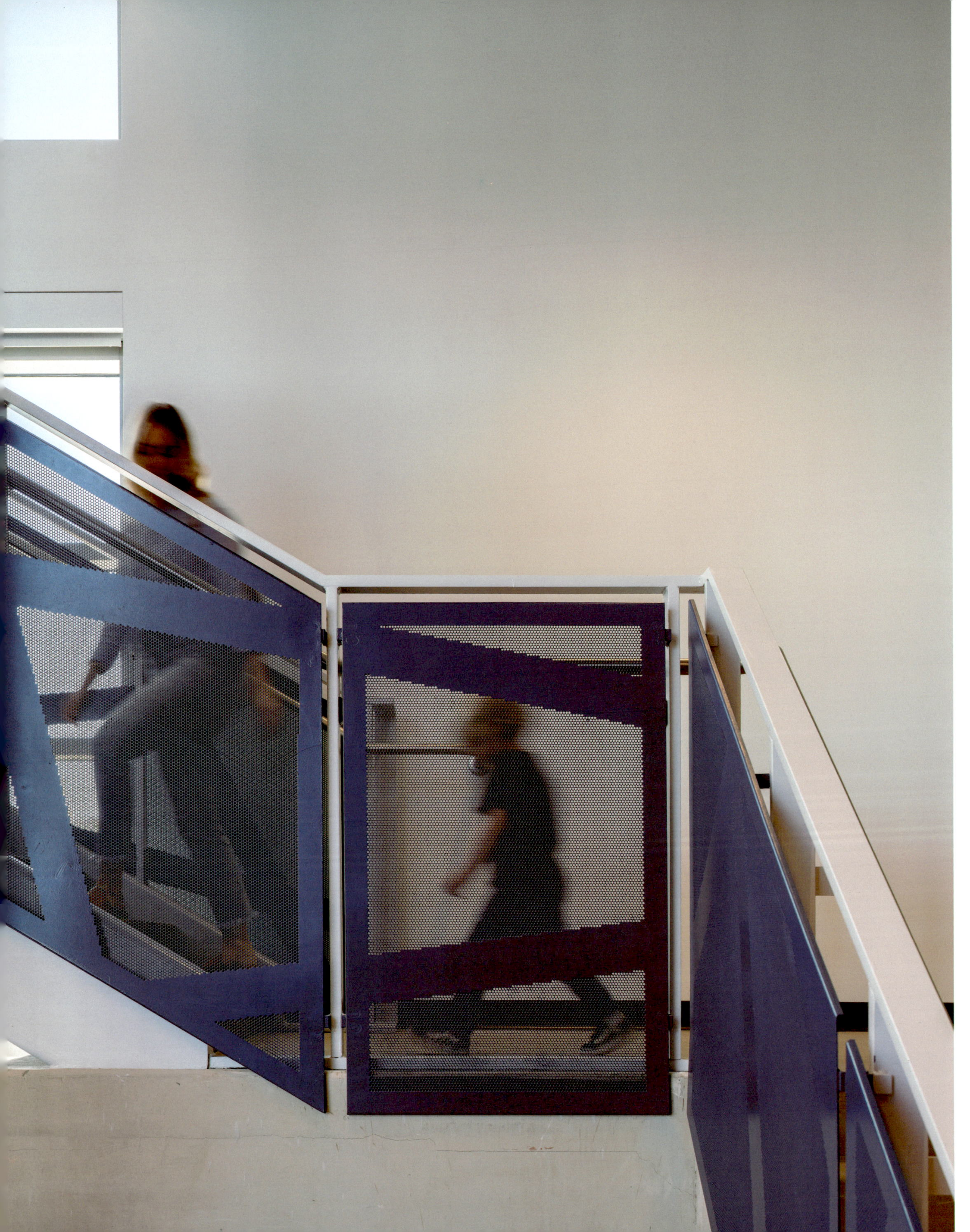

NIVERSITY UNION

Sacramento State University Union Expansion

Sacramento, California, 2019

Since its construction in 1975, the Sacramento State University Union has been considered the living room of the campus. But technological changes, code requirements, and a demand for more space called for a much-needed addition and renovation to the building. This expansion provides an improved identity for the campus while providing new meeting rooms, student lounges, retail spaces, and offices for university functions.

The original building's diagonal structural grid posed a challenge to developing a rational, efficient plan that would meet the programmatic needs of the university. In addition, grade changes around the building posed accessibility problems within the tight constraints of the site.

The design solution gives the building more permeable and light-filled spaces on the north side and a welcoming facade on the east side in a new main entry. This entry features an expansive double-height pavilion, which gives the space a grand volume that is filled with light during the day and protects visitors from the elements. The pavilion holds an outdoor gathering space with tiered seating and a wall for screening movies. It serves as the main entrance to a large coffee shop, a bicycle shop, and a graphic design studio. These retail venues help to activate the building's pedestrian zone.

A study space in the north lounge has a variety of seating and plenty of power outlets to accommodate flexible study and socialization spaces. Hexagonal acoustic cloud-like tiles provide a human scale to the space and minimize the visual impact of the exposed ceiling structure and systems.

The second floor of the north lounge is a balcony that overlooks seating for the double-height volume of the coffee shop. A large expanse of windows along with vertical sunshades allow filtered natural daylight in and views out from both the second-floor lounge and the coffee shop.

Along an open seating area at the north end of the building, a repurposed art piece separates the lounge area from circulation space and also serves as a railing. From this space a glass wall opens onto a game room. The exposed concrete walls of the original building are visible in this renovated space. They are an ever-present reminder of the history of the Sacramento State University Union and a complement to its contemporary expansion.

UNIVERSITY UNION

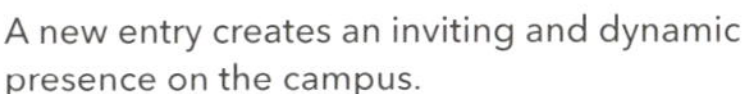

A new entry creates an inviting and dynamic presence on the campus.

UNIVERSITY UNION

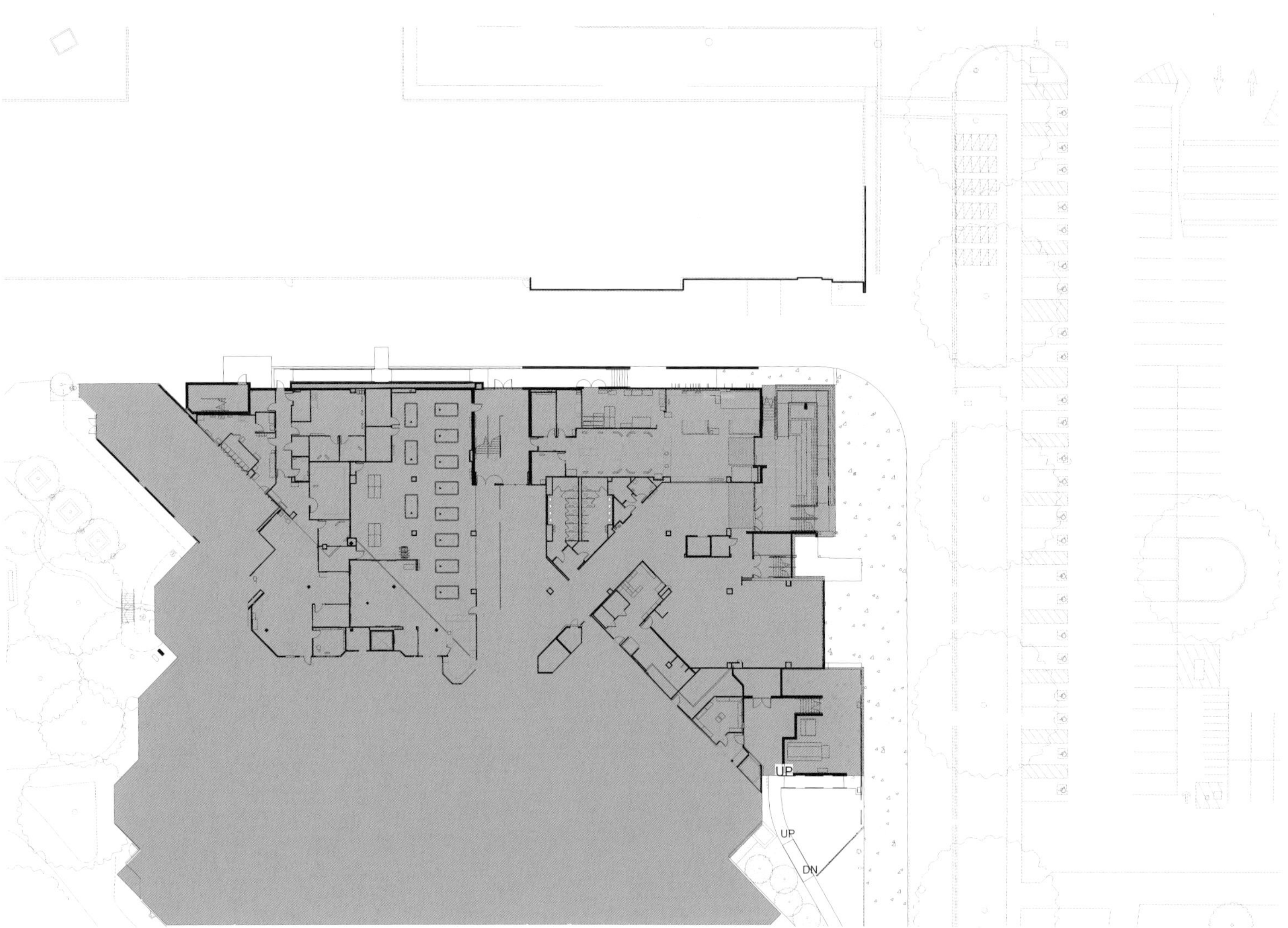

UP
UP
DN

The north facade will be a prominent edge to the future extention of the quad.

GEAR RENTALS
BIKE SHOP

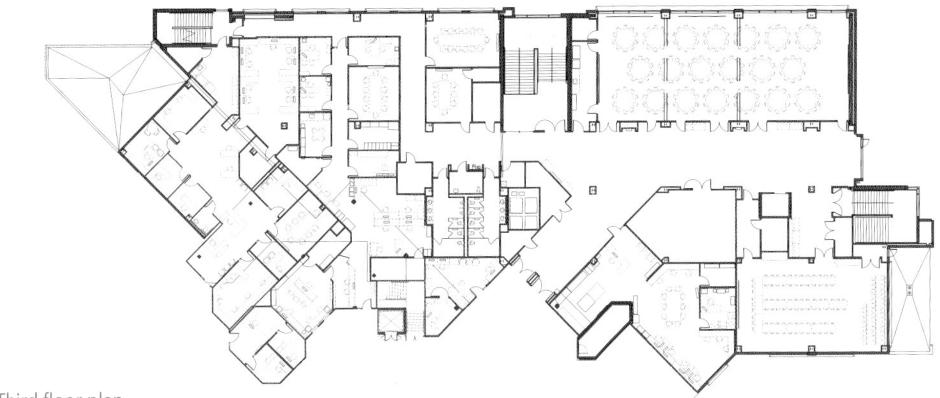

Third floor plan.

Second floor plan.

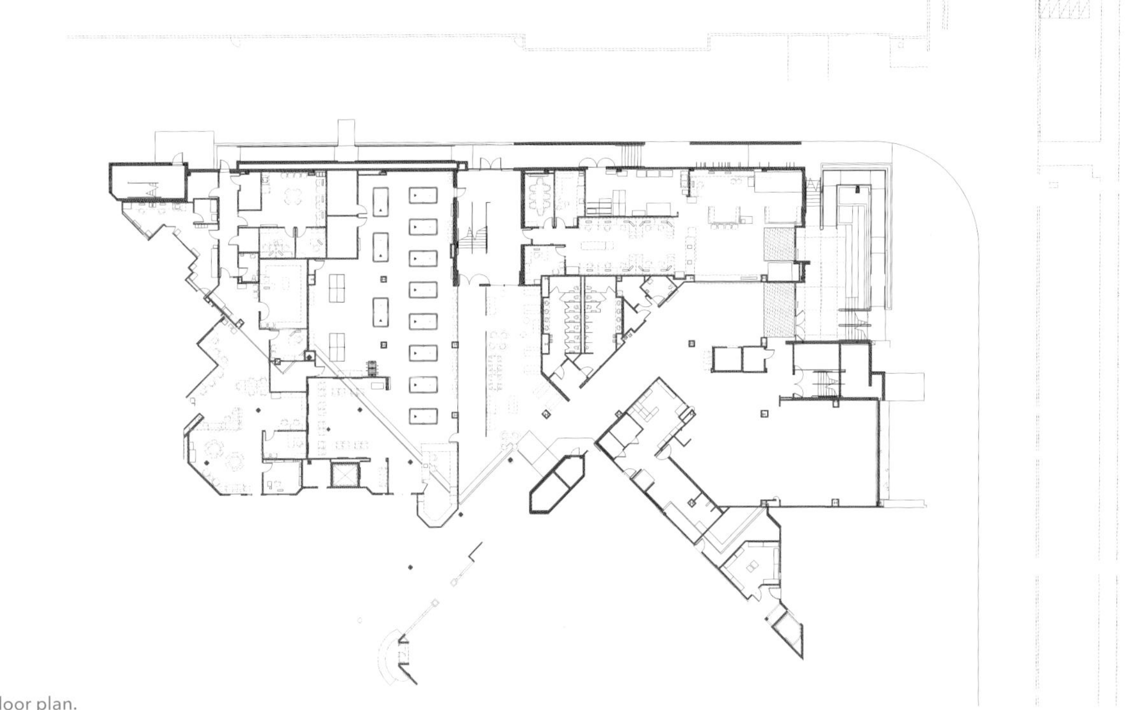

First floor plan.

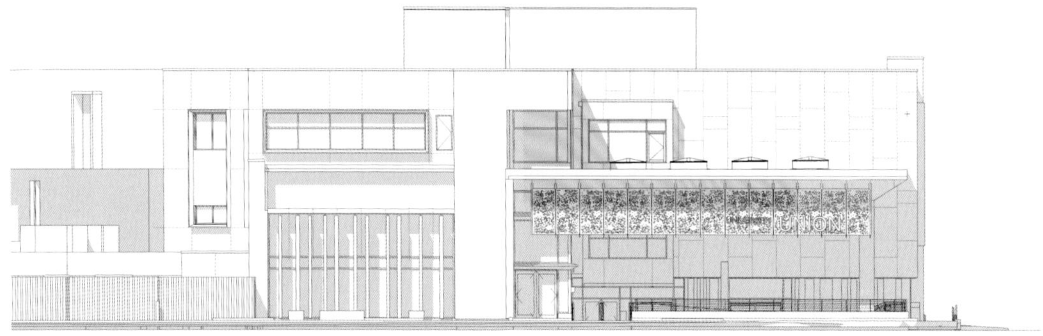

East elevation.

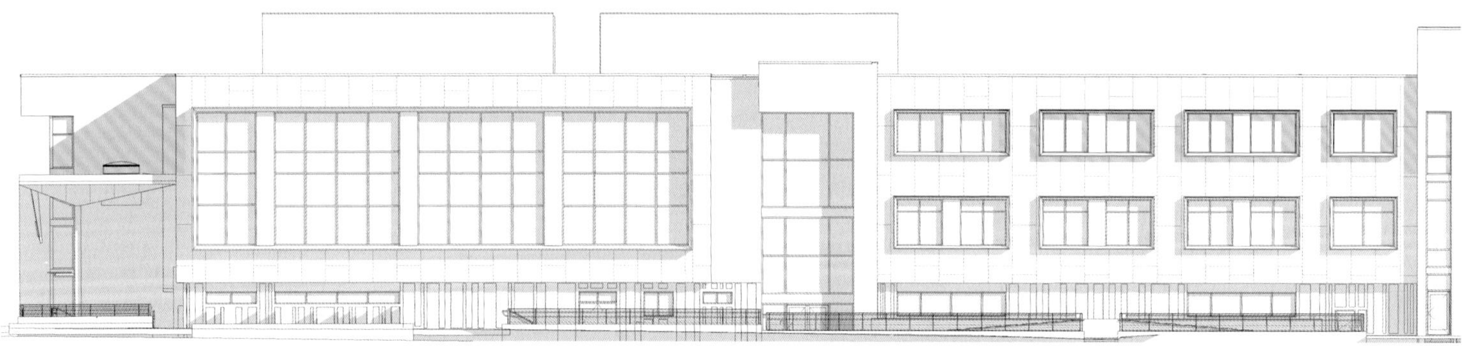

North elevation.

INFORMATION

Student lounge spaces are clearly defined to maintain logical circulation elements.

2
Cottonwood Suite

Colorful elements and forms support active environments for students.

STARBUCKS

SUNDT

UNIVERSITY UNION

Sacramento Municipal Utility District (SMUD) Headquarters Rehabilitation

Sacramento, California, 2019

In 1958, Albert M. Dreyfuss and Leonard D. Blackford designed the Sacramento Municipal Utility District (SMUD) Headquarters, and in 2014 the firm was commissioned to to renovate and rehabilitate the entire facility, inside and out. Though remarkably intact and well cared for, the building clearly needed remediation for hazardous materials and a detailed cleaning of the facade, which included artist Wayne Thiebaud's mosaic tile mural, *Water City*. In addition, concerns over water intrusion and structural performance in an earthquake–along with the desire to provide a vibrant workplace for a changing generation of workers–gave clear direction for the rehabilitation. Site and landscape improvements designed to maintain historically significant features of the thirteen-acre site were also included in this work.

To reinforce the openness of the original building, Dreyfuss + Blackford designed a carefully considered pair of additions, one on each side of the core. These allow for greatly increased daylighting and access to views. This new building area includes different types of conferencing, meeting, and break areas, successfully transforming what had been mostly unutilized spaces into an activated environment. A large open stairway replaces the original central, enclosed stairwell and mechanical shaft to allow for enhanced vertical circulation and transparency between the wings.

The addition of east- and west-facing windows presented a challenge of heat gain that was solved by using thermochromic glass. This glass is transparent until heated by direct sunlight, when it begins to darken and block the sun.

Dreyfuss + Blackford completely modernized new office areas to address the needs of SMUD's multigenerational workforce while incorporating the original design's five-foot structural grid. The original headquarters was designed to promote the use of electricity in all facets of life. The new design updates this intention; with solid-state LED lighting coupled with significant advances in energy-efficient comfort systems, the building seamlessly integrates new technology while significantly reducing energy use.

The SMUD Headquarters is on the National Register of Historic Places and the California Register of Historic Resources. Its rehabilitation achieved LEED Gold certification. Though incredibly important to the Sacramento region as a significant modernist icon, the SMUD Headquarters rehabilitation project is equally important to efforts of modernist preservation nationwide. The success of this effort, and the resulting overwhelming acceptance of it in the preservation community, serves as a shining example of what can be achieved through reverential rehabilitation of precious modernist resources.

Complete restoration of Wayne Thiebaud's 1959 *Water City* mosaic tile mural brings its vibrant colors back to life.

North Wing
Central Core
South Wing
S Street
HWY 50

Bicycle Parking
Parking
Library
Stair
Board Chambers
Waiting Area
Glass Corridor
Glass Corridor
Conf.
Conference Center
Lobby
Auditorium
Green Room

A high-efficiency LED system that is physically reminiscent of the original fluorescent solution provides uniform lighting to the Thiebaud mural.

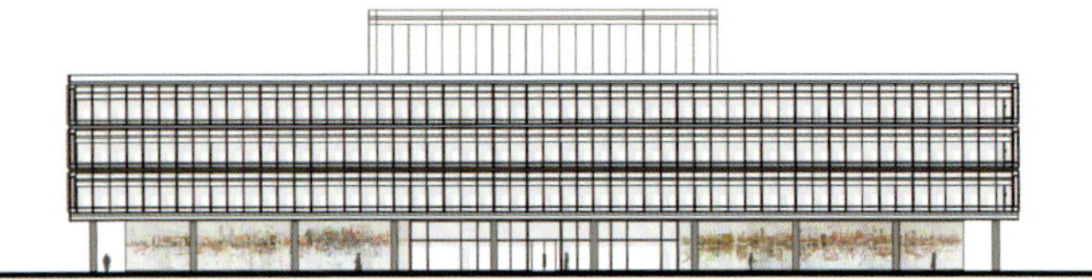

Soth elevation.

East elevation.

West elevation.

Removal of overgrown, unoriginal landscaping allows the entry to return to its original state.

UTILITY DISTRICT
6201 S STREET
Headquarters
Main Lobby
Customer Lobby
Bill Payment

The restored outdoor dining area is updated
with modern furnishings and technology.

A modern LED luminous ceiling system restores the original concept to the lobby and effectively incorporates technical systems.

New minimalist sliding glass doors between existing glass tile elements deliver transparent security.

An open and light-filled central stair that encourages use and interaction replaces an old, enclosed, dark stair.

A minimalist structural glazing system wraps part of the recessed plinth to provide code-compliant exiting and security.

EXIT

Glazed additions provide access to light and views and include needed collaboration space.

Thermochromic glass keeps these glazed spaces from incurring excess heat gain.

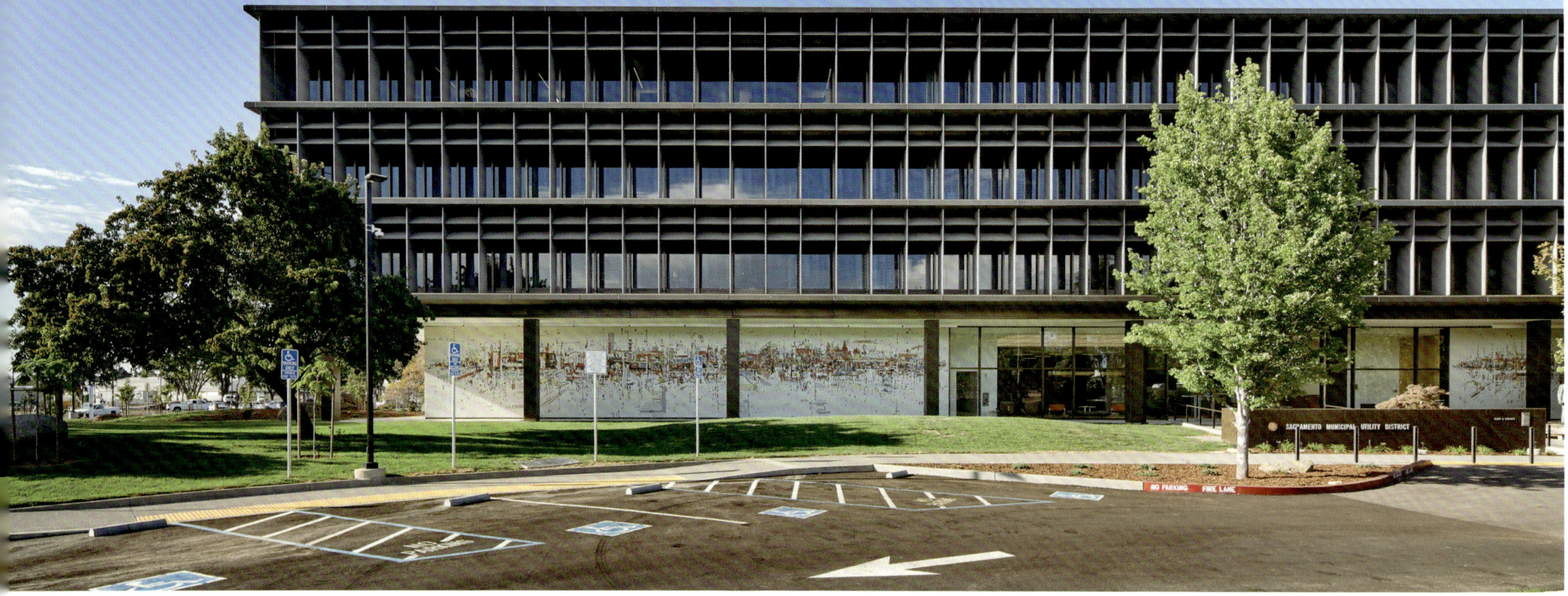

Overleaf: The building additions are clearly distinct yet compatible with the original design.

NO PARKING
NO PARKING
NO PARKING

NO PARKING

COUNTY OF SANTA CLARA
ANIMAL
SERVICES
CENTER
COUNTY OF SANTA CLARA
ANIMAL SERVICES CENTER

County of Santa Clara Animal Services Center

San Martin, California, 2021

The County of Santa Clara Animal Services Center (CSCASC) sought a new shelter to replace its current home, a converted house next to the highway. CSCASC planned to relocate to a site some distance away from the daily traffic rush and drivers' (potential adopters') eyes. While traditional municipal animal shelters grew out of a "county pound" model and evolved into showroom-like adoption centers, CSCASC needed more than just a showroom—a building that would draw attention in its now less-prominent location.

This prompted an architectural expression that would reinforce CSCASC as a destination—a design that would encourage adopters to travel there from other parts of the San Jose region. Supporting that goal, Dreyfuss + Blackford encouraged the County of Santa Clara to expand its program for CSCASC to include a large multipurpose space. This space is celebrated with a dramatic street-facing butterfly roof, a fully glazed facade, and giant hydraulic doors that open to an outside court.

Working closely with the county's staff and researching through site tours of other Northern California facilities, Dreyfuss + Blackford determined that to support the county's 95% live adoption rate—currently the highest in California—CSCASC needed to highlight every animal in its facility. Typical shelters have a showroom of pets (primarily dogs) in front and a separate space for lesser-adoptable pets in the back. They often have separated back-to-back rows of kennels, where the farther the dog is down the aisle, the less likely it is to be adopted. Steering away from this model, the team imagined: what if the dog adoption path could be a continuous loop? Along this path, visitors can view the surrounding landscape through simple expanses of full-height glass. This loop led to a new standard and opened a space in the center of the building. The resulting outdoor space added value as an exercise yard for dogs to meet their potential adopters and as a venue for hosting events.

The building massing is delineated into five sections under five gable roof forms, echoing the site. Both building and landscape are formed into a series of peaks and valleys that reflect the surrounding landforms and provide expansive surfaces for future solar power generation. The rear of the facility, where the back-of-house functions are held, has metal standing-seam roofing covering its undulating roof forms and walls. These folded metal planes open out as they approach the street, as if inviting visitors to explore the building. Ceiling planes hang horizontally throughout the building except in the community center, where they tilt upward under the butterfly roof. Visitors travel through spaces of varied scales. A courtyard and lobby allow them to pause and take their time on the journey that will hopefully result in a new family member.

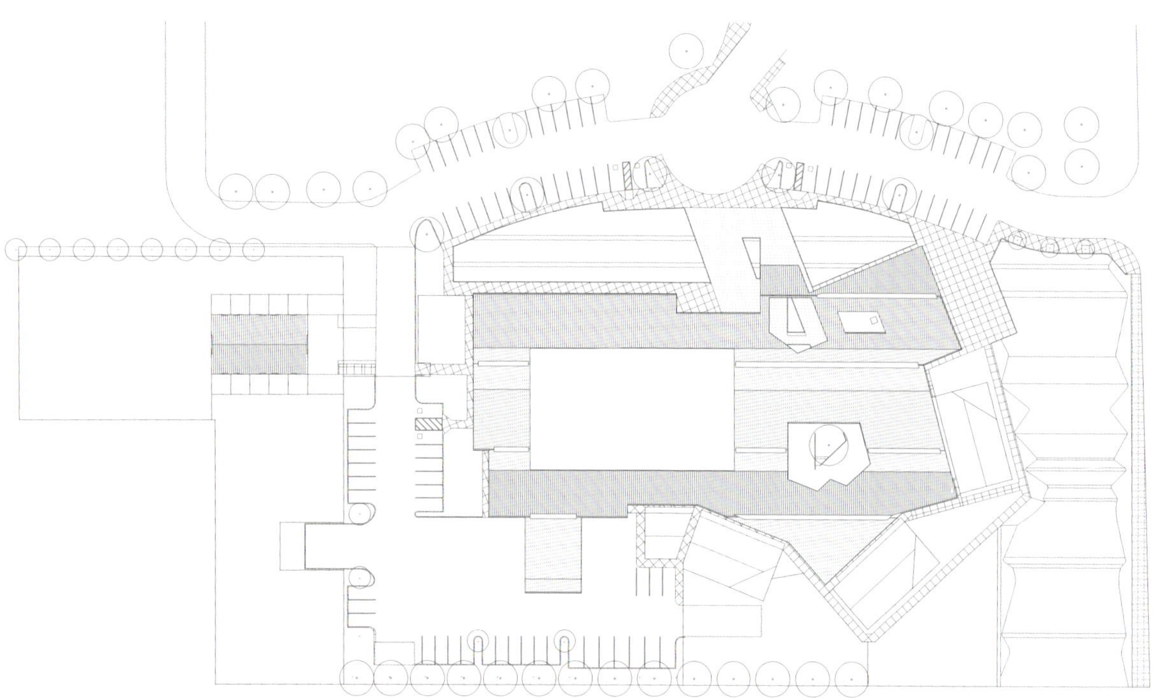

FUTURE PACKAGING

The undulating metal roof is inspired by the agrarian barn form and the surrounding mountain ranges.

An outdoor play space is surrounded by the adoption center and public spaces.

Both formal and native landscape elements produce accessory space and transitions.

ANIMAL
SERVICES
CENTER

The roof plane opens up to visitors at the entry and folds down at the rear.

Large hangar-style doors deliver access to the outdoors.

CENTER
ANIMAL
CLINIC
COUNTY OF SANTA CLARA
ANIMAL
SERVICES
CENTER

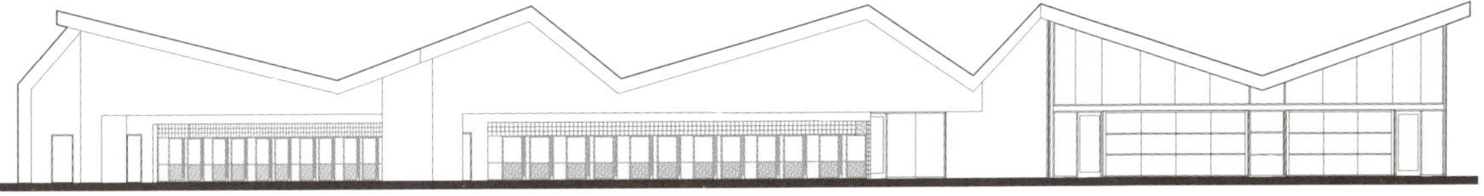

East elevation.

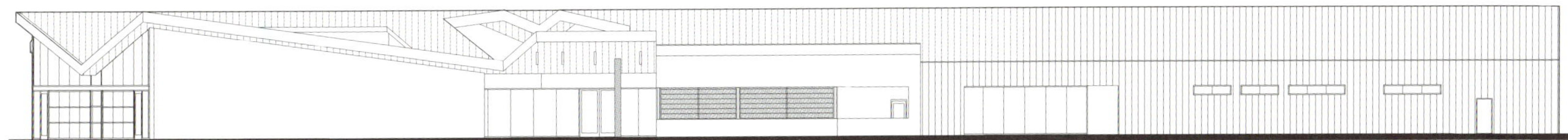

North elevation.

The folded roof plane is cut to reveal the sky at the entry and extends to a dramatic canopy.

Oversized graphics are used throughout for wayfinding and aesthetic interest.

The play space is surrounded from all sides with full-height glazing.

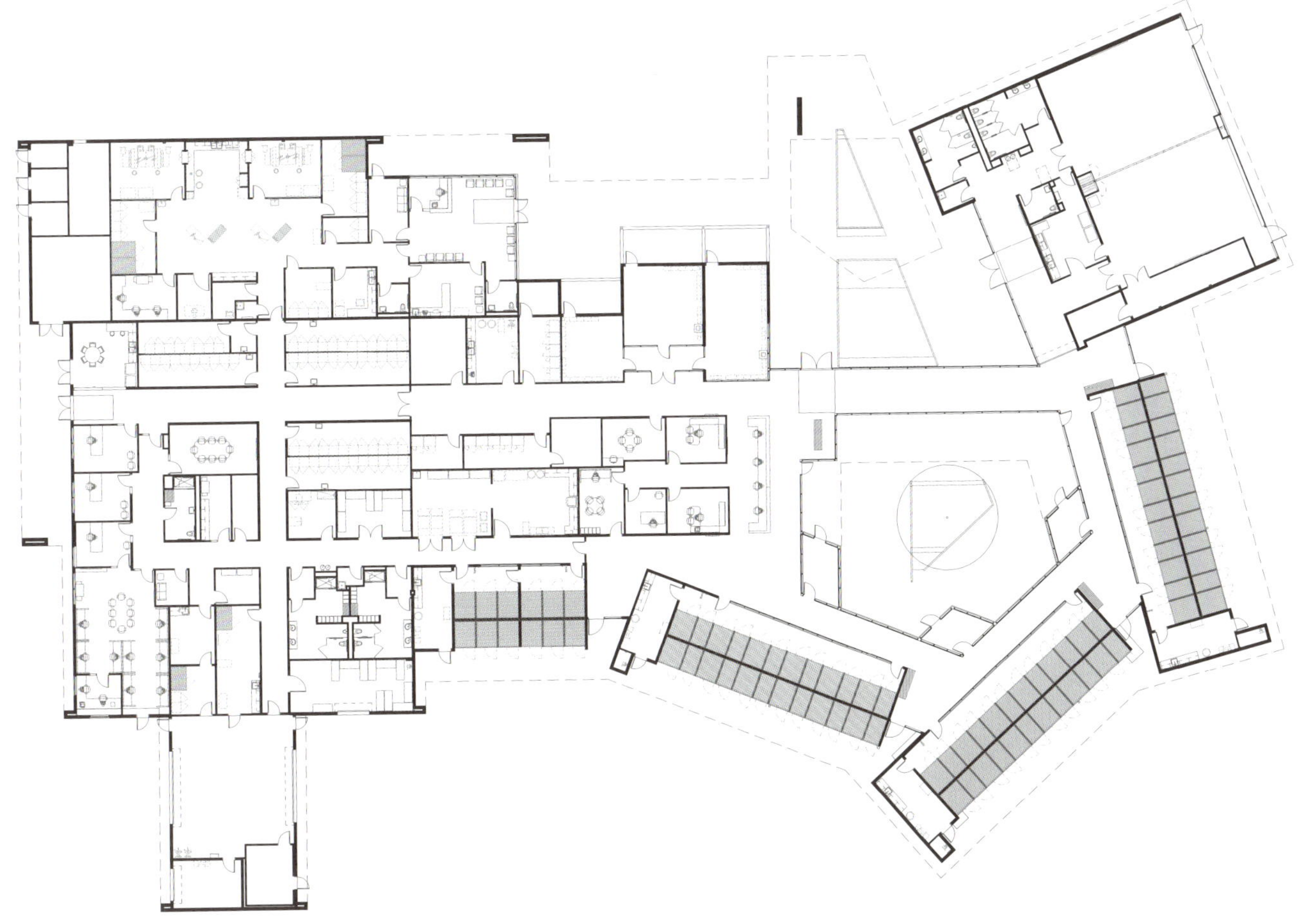

In the center of the adoption center, visitors can interact with dogs outdoors and be seen from all sides.

The roof forms create visual interest in the building's most open space.

HANG ART

Acknowledgments

The partners of Dreyfuss + Blackford Architecture would like to express thanks to those whose work has made this book possible. Many thanks to Will Smith (the other one, not the actor) for your many contributions and firm, yet understanding, shepherding of cats. Thanks also to Raquel Urbani for providing insight and support when needed, and to Brian Lefholz, Amy Eliot, Pablo Zavala, and many other staff members for contributions of support and written and graphic material.

Special thanks also go out to our collaborators. Clare Jacobson has not only provided masterful editing expertise but also has gone above and beyond in helping us move this project forward. Pablo Mandel, our talented book designer, has created an enriched visual experience that effectively expresses our personality as a firm.

Our gratitude extends also to Pierluigi Serraino. Your insights into our history and observations of our place in the world of architecture have helped us to better understand ourselves.

With seventy years behind us it seems like a good time to acknowledge all those who contributed and collectively built Dreyfuss + Blackford Architecture. This list of past and current (set in bold) staff serves as a small measure of thanks to those who have built and defined our culture and personality. Apologies for any unintended omissions in this list, and cheers to all!

Albert M. Dreyfuss
Leonard D. Blackford

Ellen Aasletten
Tony Acosta
Mario Ajello
Roy Akiyama
Jaymi Alas
Josie Aldrich
Donna Sherman Allen
Virginia Alverez
Tony Amato
Julian Andrade
Juancho Angeles
Joseph Angello
Stacy Auslam
Chris Avanzino
David Bailey
Erin Baily
Jim Ray Baker
Alex Balais
Reginald Baptiste
Shawn Barba
Gabriel Bardales
Kristopher Barkley
Corbin Barkley
Jim Barnett
Wesley Barnum
Charlie Bell
Alyssa Belluzzi
Teri Bequette
Sarah Bergman
Hugo Bianchini
Mitch Bjorgum
Richard Blackburn
Dennis Blackford
Larry Borden
Cheryl Botkin
Eloise Boyles
Bob Boylin
Tim Brown
Joshua Brown
Ethan Browning
Victor Burbank
G'Anna Burke
Gregory Cain
Nancy Callery
Lori Campbell
Michael Canevari

Joanne Carter
Sharlene Castellanos
Marilyn Castro
Catherine Chan
Mike Ching
Marie Chiu
Sophia Chun
Ilanit Cohen
Bob Collins
Jim Connerley
Larry Conrad
Jennifer Costa
Dean Costello
Tessa Couvrette
Jeannette Coveit
Bonnie Cox
Ryan Craney
Shelle Curtright
Durgesh Danait
Hayley Daniels
Don Davidson
Brent J. Davies
Heather Davis
Jay Davison
David DeRemigis
Danielle DeSilva
Carol Deering
Roland Delmendo
Keith Demaray
Anisha Deshmane
Richard Deutsch
Rupali Dogra
Roderic Dow
Gregory Durbin
Stephen Durdle
James Eastman
Amy Eliot
Richard Engler
Matthew Engstrand
David J. Evans
Gil Fabrie
Soran Faraj
Jeff Farley
George Feathers
Gus Fischer
John Frando
Rachel Freund
Jerry Fujimoto
Alex Garcia
Chad Garcia-Byrd
Aurther Gemmel
Michael Gervais
Merle Gilliland
Mark Girardi
Ted Glass
Renee Goggin
Dewitt Grow
Vanessa Gutierrez
Lori Hall
Fred Hammel
Richard Hampel
Virgil Hancock
Timothy Hannon
Paul Harding
Jack Havlick
John Head
Chase Hearn
Thomas Heffernan
Valerie Hernandez
Todd Herringer
Sheba Hill
Hieu Hoang
Christopher Holt
Fred Hummel
Hieu Huynh
Kristin Hyatt
Joseph Jackson
Christian Jacob
Vera Jansone
Kristina Jardis
Kanta Jasmine
Carol Jeannette
Shirley Johannesna
Courtney Johnson
Steven Johnson
Jane Johnson
Ray Juarez
Ken Kamada
Yuji Kaneko
Pam Kelley Faughnan
Ted Kinoshita
Kylie Kirk
George Klumb
Paul Knox
Jeff Kosinski
Jennifer Krauter
Joy Krynak
Sammie Lamont
Julie Lara
Donald Leach
Matthew Lechowick
Richard Lee
Willie Lee
Michael Lee
Woo Lee
Brian Lefholz
Francis Leighton
Tom Lemly
Robert Lempera
Carlos Leon
Audrey Lerman
Arturo Levenfeld
Allan Levy
Wyman Lewis
Gary Lewis
Philip Li
Jenny Li
Kenneth Lin
Philip Little
Larry Lockwood
Jeff Lucke
Martha Ludwig
James Macfee
Sherry Mack
Dave Madow
Terry Maiers
Carol Mandell
Melody Mar
Katie Marcyan
Michael Marquez
Peggi Martin
Anthony Martinez
Rene Marugg
Ronald Matsuoka
Bill McBreaty
James McColloch
Thomas McFall
Michael McGale
Anna McGary-Cole
Bob McLaughlin
Courtney McLeod-Golden
Carol McNeill
Ken Meyer
Kurt Micheels
Chloe Miles
Michael Monson
Hiro Morimoto

Gerald Mosely
Kenneth Murai
Edward Murray
Marcia Naff
Kristina Nedeoglo
Lorentz Nelson
Joyce Newland
Stanley Ng
Andy Noble
Tuireann O'Neill
Travis Oliver
Nancy Olson
Tracey Olsson
Chuck Olmstead
Kristi Omoto
Paul Ornealas
Esther Paik
Sugra Panvelwala
Carolyn Passmore
Edward Patton
Margie Paulsen
Paula Pertile
David Pines
Tabitha Pontino
Mary Poole Anne
Gene Porter
Jared Poulsen
Margaret Prior
Nicholas Puketza
Virender Puri
Claudia Reid
Jennifer Reid
William Reid
Marilyn Reynolds
Valerie Rhodes
Justin Ribble
Bill Richards
Kennedy Rivers
Brandin Roat
Araceli Rosas-Willett
Allan Rouse
Andre Rushton
Jaclyn Sackett
Vipul Safi
Aleta Sage
Allison Salzman
Shelby Sanders
Karin Santos
Michele L. Santos
Peter Saucerman
George Schelcher
Gary Schoenfeldt
George Schreiter
Greg Schulmeister
Brian Sehnert
Ramji Shah
Scott B. Shannon
Jason A. Silva
Stanley Silva
Jennifer Simmons
Will Smith
Carol Smith
Carl Smith
William Somyak Jr
Lisa Sperry
Ronald Steinert
Ann Stoddart
Allen Strong
Frances Strong
Stephanie Swain
Angela Swanson
Roy Swedin
Garrett Sweeden
Tarik Taeha
John Talley
Richard Tannahill
Greg Taylor
Elizabeth Ann Thompson
Duane Thompson
Ginger Thompson
Kay Tonnemacher
Erin Toves
Terry-Andrew Tremayne
John Trueblood
Raquel Urbani
David Vagg
Tony Valitas
Marco Valle
David VanZanen
Genevieve Vargas
Kyle Vargas
Pat Veda
Tony Velasco
Frank Veninga
Felinor Vidad
Jeffrey Walker
Michael Walsh
Kris Warmdahl
Jim Warner
John Webre
Ted Wener
Mark Wheeler
Richard White
Carole Whitehouse
Daphne Wiegard
Julian Wilke
Suzanne Wong
Charles Wright
David Yamane
Sharon Ybarra
Randy Yee
Jeffrey Yip
Jing Yuan
Ricardo Zamora
Pablo Zavala
James Zisch
John Zorich

Captions:
Front Cover: Window louvers, Sacramento Municipal Utility District (SMUD) Headquarters, Sacramento, California, 1960, photo by Rondal Partridge, graphic treatment by Kris Barkley and Will Smith

ii: Dreyfuss + Blackford Architecture, Sacramento Office at 3540 Folsom Boulevard, Sacramento, California, 2021, photo by Will Smith, photo treatment by Pablo Mandel

vi: Albert M. Dreyfuss's first office at 2127 J Street, Sacramento, California, 1950, photo © Dreyfuss + Blackford Architecture

viii: Night elevation, Sacramento Municipal Utility District (SMUD) Headquarters, Sacramento, California, 1960, photo by Rondal Partridge

xii: Aerial view of County of Santa Clara Animal Services Center, 2021, photo by Kyle Jeffers

xiv-xv, (clockwise from top left): Sacramento International Airport (SMF), Terminal A, 1998, photo by Cathy Kelly; Sacramento Savings and Loan, 1962, photo Sirlin Studios; Campus Commons Patio Homes, 1980, photo by Jim Mazzuchi; San Fancisco International Airport (SFO), 1970, photo by Joshua Friewald; Vogel Chevrolet Showroom, 1959, photo by Phil Fein & Associates; The Mansion Inn, 1958, photo by Roy Flamm; CalPERS Headquarters Lincoln Plaza North, 1987, photo by Kyle Jeffers

Credits:
All drawings © Dreyfuss + Blackford Architecture.
All photos © Dreyfuss + Blackford Architecture except the following:
x: Ernest Braun
xi, 3, 28, 29: Sirlin Studios
7, 10, 21, 22, 24 (top), 25, 31, 32: Joshua Friewald
8 (bottom): Pope Studios
9, 11, 14 (bottom), 18 (bottom): Phil Fein & Associates
12, 14 (top), 16, 17, 18 (top), 19 (top): Rondal Partridge
13, 15: Gordon McCampbell
19 (bottom): Courtesy of SMUD Archives
24 (bottom): Courtesy of Vacaville Museum
37, 53 (bottom): Jason A. Silva
40–45, 87, 124–128, 129 (top), 131–151, 153–159, 160 (top), 161–171: Kyle Jeffers
49: Courtesy of Sacramento International Airport
50, 51 (bottom): Cathy Kelly
51 (top): Izzy Schwartz
53 (top): Gregory Blore
54–58: David Wakely
78–79: Chip Allen
81, 82, 88–103, 105–107, 109–123: Rien van Rijthoven
104, 108: Raquel Urbani
129 (bottom), 130 (left): Courtesy of Center for Sacramento History
149, 152, 224: Will Smith
160 (bottom), 168 (bottom right): Brian Lefholz
172–197: Bruce Damonte
198–223: Tim Griffith

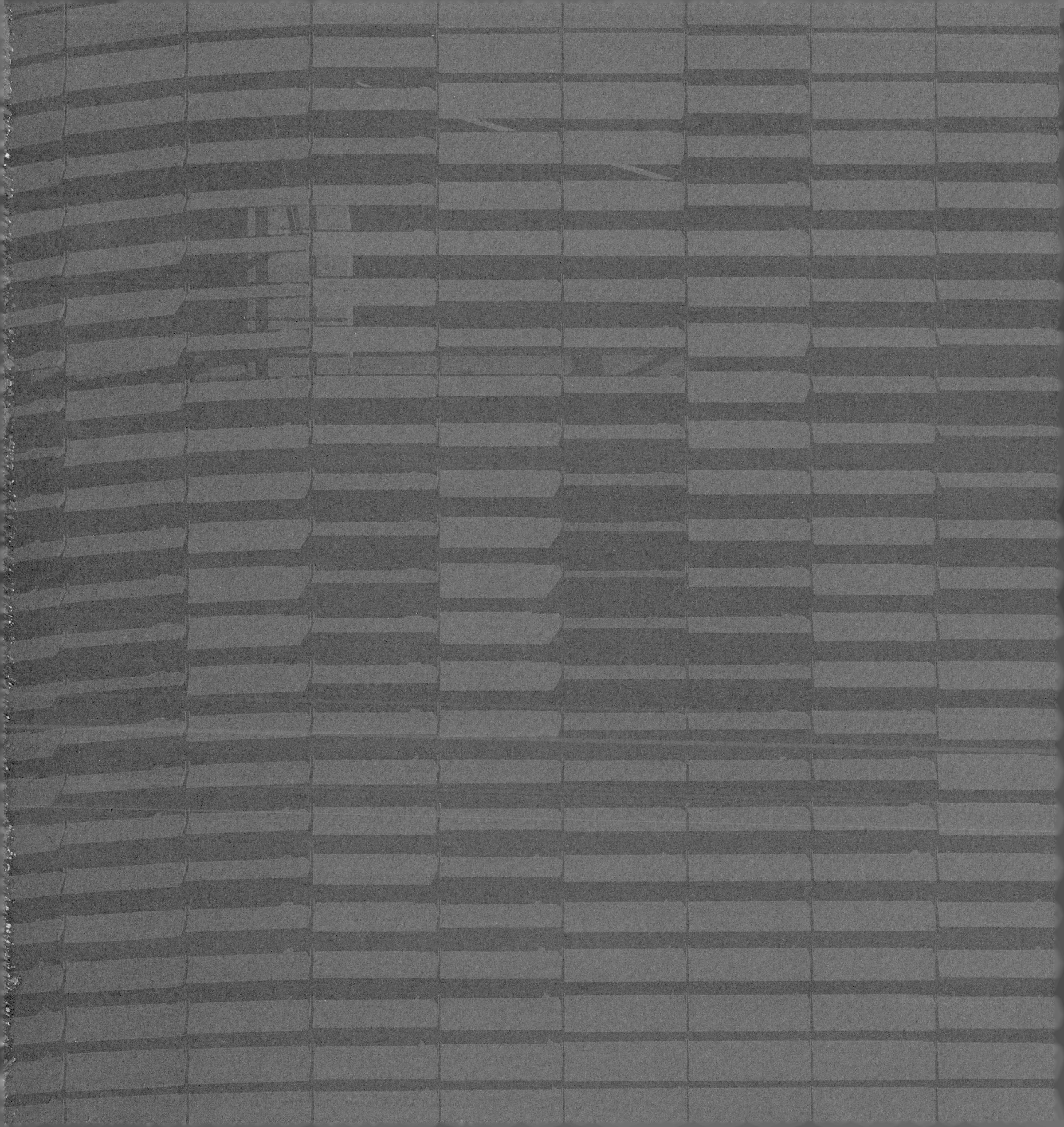